Miracle on 10th Street

By Madeleine L'Engle

Miracle on 10th Street

& Other Christmas Writings by

Madeleine L'Engle

Harold Shaw Publishers
Wheaton, Illinois

Some previously published pieces have been shortened, reformatted, retitled, or in other ways altered in order to suit the nature of this book. The reader may wish to note that some of Madeleine L'Engle's selections included here contain ideas also appearing in *The Irrational Season*.

Portions of this book have been previously published in *WinterSong: Christmas Readings by Madeleine L'Engle and Luci Shaw*. Copyright © 1996 by Harold Shaw Publishers

Copyright © 1998 by Harold Shaw Publishers

All Scripture quotations, unless otherwise indicated, are taken from *The King James Version* of the Bible.

ISBN 0-87788-531-1

Compiled by Lil Copan and Miriam Mindeman
Cover design and illustration by David LaPlaca

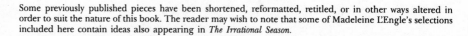

Library of Congress Cataloging-in-Publication Data

L'Engle, Madeleine.
    Miracle on 10th Street, and other Christmas writings / by
    Madeleine L'Engle.
        p.   cm.
    ISBN 0-87788-531-1
    1. Christmas—Literary collections.   I. Title
PS3523.E55M57   1998
813'.54—dc21   98-24322
                                                           CIP

04   03   02   01   00   99   98
10   9   8   7   6   5   4   3   2   1

Contents

4 Glorious Mystery 59

Advent

Advent is not a time to declare, but to listen, to listen to whatever God may want to tell us through the singing of the stars, the quickening of a baby, the gallantry of a dying man.

—from "Redeeming All Brokenness"

O Oriens

O come, O come Emmanuel
within this fragile vessel here to dwell.
O Child conceived by heaven's power
give me thy strength: it is the hour.

O come, thou Wisdom from on high;
like any babe at life you cry;
for me, like any mother, birth
was hard, O light of earth.

O come, O come, thou Lord of might,
whose birth came hastily at night,
born in a stable, in blood and pain
is this the king who comes to reign?

O come, thou Rod of Jesse's stem,
the stars will be thy diadem.
How can the infinite finite be?
Why choose, child, to be born of me?

O come, thou key of David, come,
open the door to my heart-home.
I cannot love thee as a king—
so fragile and so small a thing.

O come, thou Day-spring from on high:
I saw the signs that marked the sky.
I heard the beat of angels' wings
I saw the shepherds and the kings.

O come, Desire of nations, be
simply a human child to me.
Let me not weep that you are born.
The night is gone. Now gleams the morn.

Rejoice, rejoice, Emmanuel,
God's Son, God's Self, with us to dwell.

Redeeming All Brokenness

As we move into Advent we are called to listen, something we seldom take time to do in this frenetic world of over-activity. But waiting for birth, waiting for death—these are listening times, when the normal distractions of life have lost their power to take us away from God's call to center in Christ.

During Advent we are traditionally called to contemplate death, judgment, hell, and heaven. To give birth to a baby is also a kind of death—death to the incredible intimacy of carrying a child, death to old ways of life and birth into new—and it is as strange for the parents as for the baby. Judgment: John of the Cross says that in the evening of life we shall be judged on love; not on our accomplishments, not on our successes and failures in the worldly sense, but solely on love.

Once again, as happened during the past nearly two thousand years, predictions are being made of the time of this Second Coming, which, Jesus emphasized, "even the angels in heaven do not know." But we human creatures, who are "a little lower than the angels," too frequently try to set ourselves above them with our predictions and our arrogant assumption of knowledge which God hid even from the angels. Advent is not a time to declare, but to listen, to listen to whatever God may want to tell us through the singing of the stars, the quickening of a baby, the gallantry of a dying man.

Listen. Quietly. Humbly. Without arrogance.

In the first verse of *Jesu, Joy of Man's Desiring,* we sing, "Word of God, our flesh that fashioned with the fire of life impassioned," and the marvelous mystery of incarnation shines. "Because in the mystery of the Word made flesh," goes one of my favorite propers, for it is indeed the mystery by which we live, give birth, watch death.

When the Second Person of the Trinity entered the virgin's womb and prepared to be born as a human baby (a particular baby, Jesus of Nazareth), his death was inevitable.

It is only after we have been enabled to say, "Be it unto me according to your Word," that we can accept the paradoxes of Christianity. Christ comes to live with us, bringing an incredible promise of God's love, but never are we promised that there will be no pain, no suffering, no death, but rather that these very griefs are the road to love and eternal life.

In Advent we prepare for the coming of all Love, that love which will redeem all the brokenness, wrongness, hardnesses of heart which have afflicted us.

Born once

Born once.
That's enough.
Jesus was born once,
for us.
That's enough. That's love.
Love is once for all
for all of us.
Jesus will come
He who was once born.
He will come when he will
Love is once for all
For all. That's enough.

Life—A Gift

These are very special weeks, these weeks before Christmas, weeks of quiet waiting, weeks of remembering forty years of Christmasses with Hugh, or earlier Christmasses with my parents, weeks of affirmation that life is a gift and that what we have had we will always have, and that despite the "change and decay in all around we see" we do have a part to play in the future.

Time and Space Turned Upside Down

*A*dvent. That time of waiting, waiting even more trembling and terrible than the waiting between Good Friday and Easter Sunday.

But what are we waiting for? Why? We're not waiting, as we so often are taught as children, for Christmas, for the baby Jesus to be born in a stable in Bethlehem. We're waiting for something that has not happened yet, that has never happened before, something totally new. We know only what the end of this waiting has been called throughout the centuries: The Second Coming.

What is it, the coming of Christ in glory? The return of Christ to the earth? What's it going to be like? We don't know. We don't know anything about this event that is new, that has never before happened.

But, being human and therefore curious, we want to know. We want to know so badly that sometimes we think we do know, and that can sometimes lead to danger and even evil. Whenever we want to know something before its true time, we get into trouble. We've never learned how to wait. We're impatient creatures. Our impatience, our unwillingness to wait, is all through our stories, from Adam and Eve on.

The only thing I know about the Second Coming is that it is going to happen because of God's love. God made the universe out of love; the Word shouted all things joyfully into being because of love. The Second Coming, whenever it happens and whatever it means, will also be because of love.

We express what we believe in icons, which are creative, or idols, which are destructive. But what is a constructive icon?

Icons break time and space. One of my favorite icons is Reblev's famous picture of the Trinity, the three heavenly angels who came to visit Abraham and Sarah sitting at a table in front of the tent. On the table is the meal that has been prepared for the heavenly visitors, and what is this meal? We look at the table and see chalice and paten, the bread and the wine. Time and space turned upside down. Here, three thousand years before the birth of Christ, is the Trinity, Father, Son, and Holy Spirit; here, three thousand years before Jesus came into time for us, is the body and the blood.

So what could be an icon of the Second Coming? I think of Creation itself, and how little the astrophysicists know about it. It does seem that there was, indeed, a moment of Creation, when something, so subatomically tiny as to be almost nothing at all, suddenly opened up to become everything. How long did it take? There wasn't any time before the beginning. Time began with the beginning. Time will end at the ending, at the Second Coming.

On a rare, clear night I look at the stars. According to present knowledge, all the stars are rushing away from each other at speeds impossible for us to conceive. Are they going to keep on, getting further and further away, more and more separate? Or is there going to be a point at which the procedure is reversed, and they start coming together again? Nobody knows.

The metaphor that has come to me is birth. Our ordinary (oh, no, they're not ordinary at all—they're extraordinary) human births. Right now I am like the unborn baby in the womb, knowing nothing except the comforting warmth of the amniotic fluid in which I swim, the comforting nourishment entering my body from a source I cannot see or understand. My whole being comes from an unseen, unknown nurturer. By that nurturer I am totally loved and protected, and that love is forever. It does not end when I am precipitated out of the safe waters of the womb into the unsafe world. It will not end when I breathe my last, mortal breath. That love manifested itself joyously in the creation of the universe, became particular for us in Jesus, and will show itself most gloriously in the Second Coming. We need not fear.

There are many tough questions for which we have no finite, cut and dried answers. Even Jesus did not answer all our questions! But he came, because of that love which casts out fear. He came, and he will come again.

Even so, come Lord Jesus!

Coming, ready or not!

Luke 14:32

Coming, ready or not!
  The children freeze in their hiding places
  waiting to be found.
  They are ready.

> *When the time for the banquet*
> *came, he sent his servant to say*
> *to those who had been invited,*

Coming, ready or not!
  The old woman in the nursing home
  mumbles what she can remember
  of old prayers & hymns.
  She is ready.

> *"Come along; everything is ready now."*
> *But all alike started to make excuses.*

Coming, ready or not!
  The executive planning a meeting
  shouting for lists & faxes
  isn't ready to be ready
  not yet.

> *The first said, "I have bought a*
> *piece of land and must go and*
> *see it. Please accept my apologies."*

Coming, ready or not!
  Am I ready to be ready?
  Can I put it all down
  all the burdens
  all the needs of love
  is getting ready to be ready
  ready enough?

> *Yet another said, "I have just got*
> *married and so am unable to come."*

> *Another said, "I have bought five*
> *yoke of oxen and am on my way to try*
> *them out. Please accept my apologies."*

Coming, ready or not?
  Drop it all. Let it go.
  Let's go!
  Ready!

Advent, 1971

When will he come
and how will he come
and will there be warnings
and will there be thunders
and rumbles of armies
coming before him
and banners and trumpets
When will he come
and how will he come
and will we be ready

O woe to you people
you sleep through the thunder
you heed not the warnings
the fires and the drownings
the earthquakes and stormings
and ignorant armies
and dark closing on you
the song birds are falling
the sea birds are dying
no fish now are leaping
the children are choking
in air not for breathing
the aged are gasping
with no one to tend them

a bright star has blazed forth
and no one has seen it
and no one has wakened

Forever's Start

The days are growing noticeably shorter; the nights are longer, deeper, colder. Today the sun did not rise as high in the sky as it did yesterday. Tomorrow it will be still lower. At the winter solstice the sun will go below the horizon, below the dark. The sun does die. And then, to our amazement, the Son will rise again.

Come, Lord Jesus, quickly come
In your fearful innocence.
We fumble in the far-spent night
Far from lovers, friends, and home:
Come in your naked, newborn might.
Come, Lord Jesus, quickly come;
My heart withers in your absence.

Come, Lord Jesus, small, enfleshed
Like any human, helpless child.
Come once, come once again, come soon:
The stars in heaven fall, unmeshed:
The sun is dark, blood's on the moon.
Come, Word who came to us enfleshed,
Come speak in joy untamed and wild.

Come, thou wholly other, come,
Spoken before words began,
Come and judge your uttered world
Where you made our flesh your home.
Come, with bolts of lightning hurled,
Come, thou wholly other, come,
Who came to man by being man.

Come, Lord Jesus, at the end,
Time's end, my end, forever's start.
Come in your flaming, burning power.
Time, like the temple veil, now rend;
Come, shatter every human hour.
Come, Lord Jesus, at the end.
Break, then mend the waiting heart.

Hush!

Hush!
Wait.
What's the rush?
Why do we try to outguess God?
He will come when he comes
But nobody knows
Jesus said:
I don't know when.
Even the angels in Heaven don't know.
Only God.
Hush!
Wait.
It will be in God's time, not ours.
It will be for love
Not human chronologies.
What's a millennium?
A few years off anyhow
And on a calendar
not used by much of the world.
Hush!
Wait.
He will come for love
Never forget love
Hush!
Wait.
Listen.
Love.

Incarnation

We matter to God. We matter that much. . . . That's the whole point of it all, . . . that God cared enough to be born.

—from "Transfiguration"

The first coming

He came
    throwing off glory
    like fiery suns,
    leaving power behind,
    leaving the storms of hydrogen clouds,
    the still-forming galaxies,
    totally vulnerable
    as he emptied himself.

She took him in—
    into the deepest part of her being;
    she contained the tiny Word,
    smaller than the smallest
    subatomic particle,
    growing slowly
    from immortality into mortality,
    mother and child
    together in the greatest act of love
    the Maker could give the made.

Together they created
    immortality from mortality
    How? His father was Who?

He looked like any child
    from the vulnerable top
    of his tiny skull
    to the little curling toes.

This whispered Word made
    the sun and stars,
    wind and water,
    planets and moons, and all of us.
    But he left this joy
    to be

God With Us!
    understanding lowly shepherds
    and two old people in the Temple.
    Later, three wise men—
    one from each human race—
    came, pondering.
    Most of the powerful people
    were skeptical at best
    God become Son of Man? Nonsense.

Christ will come,
    expected or unexpected,
    when God is ready,
    even while we are loudly demanding
    signs and proofs
    which close our hearts and minds
    to the Wildness of Love.

Word of Love,
    enter our hearts
    as you entered the virgin's womb.
    Come, Lord Jesus!

Transfiguration

ister Egg left the convent with the shopping cart. Over her simple habit she wore a heavy, hooded woolen cape. Even so, she shivered as the convent door shut behind her and she headed into the northeast wind. There was a smell of snow in the air, and while it would be pleasant to have a white Christmas, she dreaded the inevitable filthy drifts and slush that would follow a city snow. She dreaded putting on galoshes. But she would enjoy doing her share of shoveling the snow off the sidewalk.

The twenty-five-pound turkey was waiting in the pantry, but she needed to get cranberries and oranges for relish, and maybe even some olives to go with the celery sticks. There's only one Christmas a year, and it needs to be enjoyed and celebrated. She pulled her cape more closely about her. In her mind she started counting the weeks till August. The first two weeks of August were her rest time, when she went to her brother's seaside cottage and swam in the ocean, and for her that time was always transfigured and gave her strength to come back to the Upper West Side of New York City.

"Hi, Sister Egg!" It was the small child of the Taiwanese shopkeeper from whom she always bought garlic because he had the best garlic in the city. The child rushed at her and leaped into her arms, pushing the empty market cart aside. Sister Egg caught the little boy, barely managing not to fall over backward, and gave him a big hug. "Whatcha doing?" the little boy asked.

"Christmas shopping."

"Presents?"

"No. Food. Goodies." And she reached into her pocket and drew out one of the rather crumbly cookies she kept there for emergencies such as this. The little boy stuffed the cookie into his mouth, thereby rendering himself speechless, and Sister Egg walked on. The vegetable stand she was heading toward was across Broadway, so she turned at the corner and crossed the first half of the street; then the light turned red, so she stopped at the island. In Sister Egg's neighborhood islands ran down the center of Broadway, islands that were radiant with magnolia blossoms in the spring, followed by tulips, and delicately leafing trees. By August the green was dull and drooping from the heat. In December all the branches were bare and bleak.

She stood on the island, waiting for the light to change. She, too, felt bare and bleak. She felt in need of hope, but of hope for what she was not sure. She had long since come to terms with the fact that faith is not a steady, ever flowing stream but that it runs over rock beds, is sometimes dry, sometimes overflows to the point of drowning. Right now it was dry, dryer than the cold wind that promised snow.

"Hi, Sister Egg." She turned to see a bundle of clothes on one of the benches reveal itself to be an old woman with her small brown dog on her lap, only the dog's head showing, so wrapped were woman and dog in an old brown blanket.

"Hello, Mrs. Brown." Sister Egg tried to smile. It was Christmas Eve, and no one should spend it wrapped in an inadequate blanket, sitting on a bare island on upper Broadway. But she had learned long ago that she could not bring every waif and stray she saw out in the streets back to the convent. It was not that anybody thought it was a bad idea; it was just that the Sisters were not equipped to handle what would likely be hundreds of people hungry in body and spirit. They had taken pains to learn of every available shelter and hostel, and the hours of all the soup kitchens.

Sister Egg had tried to get this particular old woman into a home for the elderly with no success. Mrs. Brown had her share of a room in a Single Room Occupancy building. She had her dog and her independence and she was going to keep both.

From the opposite bench came a male voice, and another bundle of clothes revealed itself to be a man whose age was anybody's guess. "Sister *what?*"

"Oh—" Sister Egg looked at him, flustered.

"Sister Egg," the old woman announced triumphantly.

"Sister Egg! Whoever heard of a Sister named Egg? What are you, some kind of nut?" The scowl took over the man's body in the ancient threadbare coat as well as his face, which was partly concealed by a dark woolen cap.

Sister Egg's cheeks were pink. "My real name is Sister Frideswide. People found it hard to pronounce, so I used to say that it was pronounced 'fried,' as in fried egg. So people got to using Egg as a nickname."

"What idiot kind of a name is Frideswide?" The man's scowl seemed to take up the entire bench.

"She was an abbess in Oxford, in England, in the eighth century."

"What's an abbess?" The man sounded as though he would leap up and bite her if her answer didn't satisfy him.

"She's—she's someone who runs—runs a religious order," Sister Egg stammered.

"So what else about her?"

Did he really want to know? And how many times had the light already turned to green? And she was cold. "She was a princess, at least that's what I was told, and she ran away rather than be coerced into a marriage she didn't want."

"So she married God instead?"

"Well. Yes, I guess you could put it that way." What an odd man.

"And merry Christmas to you," he said.

She looked up just as the light changed from green to yellow to red. Wishing him merry Christmas in return was obviously not the right thing to do. She hesitated.

"And give me one reason why it should be merry. For me. For her." He jerked his chin in the direction of the old woman.

Why, indeed, should it be merry? Sister Egg wondered. There were thousands homeless and hungry in the city. Even though soup kitchens would be open for the holidays, and although volunteers would make an attempt at serving a festive meal, the atmosphere of a soup kitchen, usually in a church basement, was bleak. A basement is a basement is a basement, even with banners and Christmas decorations.

"Well?" the man demanded.

"I'm not sure it's supposed to be merry," Sister Egg said. "I'm not sure when 'merry' came into it. It's a time to remember that God came to live with us."

"That was pretty stupid," the man said. "Look where it got him."

Mrs. Brown's face peered out of the old blanket. "You hadn't ought to talk like that."

A young man on a bicycle rode through the red light. He carried a large transistor radio which blared out, "Joy to the world! the Lord is come!"

"Joy, joy, joy." The man spat the words out. "What good did it do, this Lord coming? People were bad then, and they aren't any better now. Fighting. Bombing. Terrorism."

"You're upsetting Sister," Mrs. Brown said.

Sister Egg watched the light change yet again from green to yellow to red. "It's all right," she told Mrs. Brown. "Really it's all right."

"What's all right?" the man demanded.

"It's all right to say what you feel. Only—"

"Only what?"

"I don't have any answers for you."

"Thank God," the man said.

Sister Egg smiled. "Do you?"

"Well . . . no. Thank *you*."

Sister Egg shivered. "I really have to make the next light."

"You're not warmly enough dressed," Mrs. Brown chided.

"Oh, I'm fine, as long as I keep moving."

The man stood up, and Mrs. Brown's little dog barked.

"Shut up, mutt. What're you doing tonight, Sister?"

If she heard the suggestiveness in his voice, Sister Egg gave no sign. "We always go to the cathedral for midnight mass. Are you coming, Mrs. Brown?"

"Sure," the old woman said. "I been coming since you first told me it was okay. Beautiful. All those candles. And the music. And people smiling and being nice."

"Yeah, and they come around with silver plates and expect you to put all your money in."

"Sister Egg puts in something for me," Mrs. Brown said. "Anyhow, you don't have to pay God."

"Yeah? And who pays for all those candles? You got to pay somebody."

The light changed to green. Sister Egg fumbled in her deep pocket. It would never do to give the man one of the crumbled cookies. Then her fingers touched something more solid, and her fingers pulled out a silver-foil-wrapped chocolate kiss. She dropped it in his lap, then started across the street, feeling herself flush as she heard him making smacking kissing noises after her.

I should have had some answers for him, she thought. *I should have known what to say.*

A flake of snow brushed her cheek. She hurried to her favorite vegetable store and bought cranberries and oranges and some good celery for celery sticks, and a bunch of celery that had been marked down and a bag of onions for the turkey stuffing.

"Merry Christmas, Si'r Egg." The Korean man at the cash register greeted her, and charged her half price for the oranges.

She would have to hurry. Christmas Eve Vespers and the blessing of the crib was at five, and the chapel would be full of children from the school, and parents, too, and there would be hot, spiced cider afterward, and cookies.

It was always a special time for the children. They sat through the singing of Vespers, restless, but then there was the procession to the crèche, with the shepherds adoring, and the wise men still far off, because they couldn't arrive till Twelfth Night. And food! In half an hour the cookie plates would be empty, and the Sisters had been baking for weeks.

What did the children think? Was it all cookies and fruitcake and presents? Did they think at all about God coming to live with human beings as a human being, or was it only a baby in a manger? Did they see the shadow of the cross, and failure, thrown darkly across the golden singing of the angels?

Hearts were hard two thousand years ago. Hearts were still hard.

She started to cross Broadway again, but the light had already been green when she started so, again, she was stopped at the island.

Mrs. Brown was gone. That was all right. She would see her after the midnight mass.

But the man was there.

And she still had no words of comfort. For him. For herself.

"Take me there," the man said.

Startled, she nearly dropped the bag of onions. "Where?"

"To the church. The cathedral."

It was not far. One block south, one block east. But there was no time. "Mother Cat won't like it if I'm late," she started.

"Mother *what?*" he roared.

"Oh—Mother Catherine of Siena."

"Is there a Sister Hen and a Mother Dog? Do you all have idiot nicknames?"

"Oh, no, and we don't *call* her Mother Cat, you know, it's Mother Catherine of—"

"But she calls you Egg?"

"Sometimes it's Frideswide."

He snorted. Rose. "Let's go."

"But—"

"Here. I'll carry your bags." He took the heaviest one, which contained the cranberries and oranges.

She could leave him. She was quite capable of saying, "I'm sorry, I can't be late for Vespers." She could direct him to the cathedral, she—

"Hi, Sister Egg." It was Topaze, one of the children who was in the school. His father was in and out of jail. His mother looked as though if she spat, nails could come out of her mouth. Topaze looked like an angel. "Can I carry your bags?"

"You know I can't pay you anything, Topaze," she said. The child picked up quarters and occasionally a dollar by doing errands.

"Hey, Sister Egg, merry Christmas!" And he took the bags out of her arms, leaving her empty handed. "Where're we going?"

"To the cathedral," she said. "Mr., uh—I don't know your name."

"Joe," the man said.

"Mr. Joe wants to go to the cathedral. If you'll carry the bags to the convent and give it to one of the Sisters, you won't be late for Vespers."

"What about you?" Topaze asked.

"I guess I'll be late. Tell them not to worry about me, Topaze. I'll come as soon as I can."

"Unh unh, Sister Egg. I'm staying with you and Joe. Merry Christmas, Joe."

"Merry yourself." Once again Joe's scowl seemed larger than his body. "Let's go."

Sister Egg knew that Topaze didn't want to miss Vespers. Nevertheless she was glad to have him accompanying her, especially when they turned off brightly lit Broadway to the much darker east-bound street.

The cathedral loomed at the far end, the large and handsome lamps in front of it brightly lit. Another flake brushed Sister Egg's face, but the snow had not really begun yet; there was just an occasional flake drifting down from the low clouds.

People were already starting up the steps in small groups, to be sure of finding seats, even though they would have to wait for hours. A few greeted Sister Egg. Topaze walked on her left, holding her hand. Joe walked on her right, his threadbare coat hanging loosely. But his feet did not shuffle and his scowl was fierce.

They walked up the steps, an odd trio, Sister Egg thought, and she felt a wave of compassion flow out of her and over the man whose coat had once seen very much better days. The boy squeezed her hand.

Once they were in the vast nave of the cathedral, they stopped and looked around. The clusters of people hurrying forward to claim seats seemed small and few in that enormous space. Both sides of the nave were lined with bays, small chapels in themselves. There was a bay for St. Francis, a bay for education, a bay where a long-dead bishop was buried. Joe stopped at the bay of the Transfiguration, where there was an enormous painting that had been given the cathedral, of Jesus, James, John, and Peter on the Mount of Transfiguration. Jesus' face and garments were brilliant even in the semi-darkness of the cathedral, but through and behind him was the shadow of a cross. Depending on the angle at which one looked at the picture, Jesus was transfigured with light, or his outstretched arms were on the cross. It was a stunning painting, and the bay was one of Sister Egg's favorites.

Joe put his hand against his chest, and his scowl became a grimace. "Water," he choked. "I need water."

"Topaze." Sister Egg pushed the boy in her urgency. "You know where to go. Hurry to the choir rooms and get a glass of water, quickly." Perhaps Joe needed food, too. His face was not gray. She did not think he was having a heart attack.

As soon as Topaze had put the bags of groceries down at Sister Egg's feet and vanished into the shadows, Joe braced himself against one of the stone columns of the bay, then reached out and grabbed Sister Egg's wrist. "Don't scream. Don't try to run. Give it to me."

"What?" She tried to pull away from his grasp, not understanding.

"Your money. I know you have some. You didn't spend it all on two bags of groceries."

For this she was going to be late for Christmas Eve Vespers. Even if Mother Cat—Mother Catherine of Siena—was not angry with her, the other Sisters would be. Sister Egg was always late, always stopping to speak to people.

"Come on, Egg," Joe said.

She was angry. "Couldn't you even call me a good egg?" She demanded. "Couldn't you just have asked me for it? 'Sister, I need money.' That's all you'd have needed to say."

"I don't ask for things."

"I only have a couple of dollars left. You're welcome to them." With her free hand she reached into her pocket. Pulled out a handful of crumbling cookies. "Here." Three more chocolate kisses.

"Come off it." He let her wrist go but reached for her pocket, putting his hand in and turning the pocket inside out. A small wooden cross fell to the stone floor. Some knotted woolen prayer beads. A can opener. A dog biscuit. A tiny sewing kit. "Holy— What are you, a walking dimestore?"

She looked past his head to the painting of Jesus, and now all she saw was the man on the cross. The body of the dying Christ was richly muscled. It was a strong man who hung there. Joe moved toward her impatiently, and his face came between Sister Egg and Jesus, and by some trick of the dim lighting in the nave, Joe's face looked like that of the man on the cross.

"Well, there you are," she said.

He pulled two dollars and a few coins out of her turned-out pocket. "It's not enough."

"Oh yes it is," she said. "It's more than enough." She gestured toward the painting. "God cared enough to come and be one of us, and just once during his life on earth he revealed his glory. We matter to God. We matter that much."

"Don't shout," Joe growled.

"That's why it's merry Christmas." She hardly heard him. "Not that he died. But that he cared enough to be born. That's the whole point of it all. Not the Crucifixion and the Resurrection but that God cared enough to be born. That was the real sacrifice. All the power and glory of all the galaxies—" Again she waved her arm toward the painting, and now she could not see the cross, only the glory.

She stopped for breath as Topaze hurried up with a glass of water.

Joe said, "Give it to Sister Fried Egg. She needs it more than I do."

Topaze looked at them suspiciously.

"We matter that much," Sister Egg repeated wonderingly.

Joe said, "She spilled some stuff. Help her pick it up." Two dollar bills floated to the floor. Coins dropped.

Topaze squatted and picked up Sister Egg's assorted treasures, then slipped them, one by one, into her pocket.

Joe handed him the remains of the cookies. "Here, kid, these are for you. I'll keep these." His open hand held three silver-foil-wrapped chocolate kisses. Light from somewhere in the cathedral touched them so that the silver was bright.

Sister Egg found that she was holding a glass of water.

When she turned to Joe, he was gone. She saw only the back of a man in a worn coat walking away.

"You all right?" Topaze asked anxiously. "You want the water?"

She took a sip. She could shout, "Thief!" and someone would stop Joe. Her wrist was sore where he had grabbed her. He was not a nice man.

She looked again at the painting. The face on the cross was Joe's. She turned so that the light shifted, and she saw the transfigured Christ.

"If we hurry," she said to Topaze, "we may miss Vespers, but we'll get there for the blessing of the crèche and the baby in the stable."

What Have We Done to Christmas?

Christmas! God, leaving power and glory and coming to live with us, powerless, human, mortal. What have we done to Christmas?

Story

When we try to define and over-define and narrow down, we lose the story the Maker of the Universe is telling us in the Gospels. I do not want to explain the Gospels; I want to enjoy them.

And that is how I want to read and write story. This does not mean that story deals only with cheeriness, but that beneath the reality of life is the rock of faith. I ask God to set me upon a rock that is higher than I so that I may be able to see more clearly, see the tragedy and the joy and sometimes the dull slogging along of life with an assurance that not only is there rock under my feet, but that God made the rock and you and me, and is concerned with Creation, every galaxy, every atom and subatomic particle. Matter *matters*.

This is the promise of the Incarnation. Christ put on human matter, and what happens to us is of eternal, cosmic importance. That is what true story affirms.

Creed

In the creed, as I say it each day, I affirm that "I believe in the resurrection of the body." We don't know how that body is going to be resurrected, or what it is going to be like. But if the apostle Paul could believe in a *spiritual body* so, most of the time, can I. It is yet another mystery of the Word made flesh.

By whatever name it is called—creed, affirmation, or statement of faith—most religious establishments express what they believe in one way or another. And these expressions are all inadequate. What we hold in common is the affirmation of our faith in the mystery of the Word made flesh.

When Paul was asked for explanations, his wonderful (and sensible) reply was, "Don't be silly."

In Human Flesh

The enfleshing of the Word which spoke the galaxies made the death of that Word inevitable. All flesh is mortal, and the flesh assumed by the Word was no exception in mortal terms. So the birth of the Creator in human flesh and human time was an event as shattering and terrible as the *eschaton*. If I accept this birth I must accept God's love, and this is pain as well as joy because God's love, as I am coming to understand it, is not like human love.

This birth has death forevermore confused

This birth has death forevermore confused.
That God, the holy & immortal one
Should take on mortal flesh, should be abused,
Be killed—oh, how could such a thing be done?
What does this death then do to death?
Death grasps the holy body of the Lord,
Crushes the mortal flesh, lets side be gored—
Oh, God! has death not triumphed over life?
Why did you come to share our joy & pain?
Our feeble times of peace, our constant strife?
What did you think your fragile folk might gain?
I do not know the answer, Lord, but you,
Embracing death, made life forever new.

Impossible Things

In Lewis Carroll's *Alice's Adventures Through the Looking Glass*, the White Queen advises Alice to practice believing six impossible things every morning before breakfast. It's good advice. Unless we practice believing in the impossible daily and diligently, we cannot be Christians, those strange creatures who proclaim to believe that the Power that created the entire universe willingly and lovingly abdicated that power and became a human baby.

Particle physics teaches us that energy and matter are interchangeable. So, for love of us recalcitrant human creatures, the sheer energy of Christ changed into the matter of Jesus, ordinary human matter, faulted, flawed, born with the seed of death already within the flesh as a sign of solidarity with our mortality.

But this birth also promises us that our human, mortal matter is permeated with Christ's total energy, the creative energy which shouted into being all the galaxies, hydrogen clouds, solar systems, planets, all life—even us! When Christ was born as Jesus, born of a human mother as all babies are born, that incredible birth honored all our births, and assured us that we, God's beloved children, partake of eternal life. For indeed it follows that as Christ partook of human life, we partake of the divine life.

How can we trivialize the Incarnation as we have done? Tawdry tinsel and crowded shopping malls are not the worst of it. Arguing about Christ's divinity versus Jesus' humanity is equally to miss the point. Like the White Queen we need merrily to accept the impossible (with us it is impossible; with God nothing is impossible!): The baby who was born two thousand years ago in Bethlehem was God, come to us as a human babe. Jesus: wholly human. It's more than our puny minds can comprehend. It's one reason Jesus kept insisting that we be as little children, because we can understand this wonder only with childheartedness, not with grown-up sophistication.

We can, to some extent, understand Jesus' humanity. We can glory in but not understand, in any cognitive way, his divinity. We are still like that fetus in the womb, comfortably swimming around in the warm amniotic fluid, with no idea of what life out of the womb is going to be like. Unlike us grown-ups, the fetus seems to enjoy *being* without questions! Questions are fine as long as we do not insist on finite answers to questions which are infinite. How could Jesus be wholly God and wholly human? What does the resurrection of the body mean? How can God be good if terrible things are allowed to happen? How much free will do we have? Can we make a difference?

To that last question, at least, we can say Yes, and that Yes is easier for us to say because of Christmas. What a difference this birth makes to our lives! God, in human flesh, dignifies our mortal flesh forever. How did the schism between flesh and spirit ever come about to confuse and confound us? God put on our flesh and affirmed its holiness and beauty. How could we ever have fallen for the lie that spirit is good and flesh is evil? We cannot make our flesh evil without corrupting spirit, too. Both are God's and both are good, as all that our Maker made is good.

God created, and looked on Creation, and cried out, It is good!

At Christmastime we look at that tiny baby who was born in Bethlehem, and we, too, may cry out, It is good! It is very good!

Maker of the galaxies

O Maker of the galaxies,
Creator of each star,
You rule the mountains & the seas,
And yet—oh, here you are!

You ride the fiery cherubim
And sail on comet fall.
You teach the seraphim to hymn,
And yet—you left it all.

You left the realms of fire & ice.
Into a young girl's womb you came.
O God! *This* was the sacrifice!
Nothing will ever be the same.

A Galaxy, a Baby

The birth of my own babies (every woman's Christmas) shows me that the power which staggers with its splendor is a power of love, particular love. Surely it takes no more creative concentration to make a galaxy than a baby. And surely the greatest strength of all is this loving willingness to be weak, to share, to give utterly.

That Newness

The second Christmas of our marriage, and the first with our six-month-old baby, the beautiful flesh of our child made the whole miracle of incarnation new for me, and that newness touched on *kairos* (God's time, not human time).

Now, all these years later, I plunge into the delightful business of painting Christmas ornaments with my grandchildren; I hear the hammer as Bion puts together a dolls' house which looks remarkably like Crosswicks, our house in the country; the New York kitchen smells fragrant with Christmas cookies; this, for me, is incarnation.

Epiphany

I cannot go back to night.

O Truth, O small and unexpected thing,

You have taken so much from me.

How can I bear wisdom's pain?

But I have been shown: and I have seen.

—*from "One king's epiphany"*

Miracle on 10th Street

snapshot of a little girl, a piano, a Christmas tree. What could be more ordinary, more normal, more safe? But it wasn't safe that Christmas. It might have been ordinary and normal, because what happened to us happens to many people, but it wasn't safe!

This little girl, our first child, is looking wistfully at the tree, and her usual expression was vital, mischievous, full of life. But that Christmas she was wilted, like a flower left too long without water. She sat with her toy telephone and had long, quiet conversations with her lion ("You can never talk while the lion is busy," she would explain). She didn't run when we took her to the park. She was not hungry. I bathed her and felt her body, and there were swollen glands in her groin, her armpits.

We took her to the doctor. He looked over our heads and used big medical words. I stopped him. "What you are saying is that you think she has leukemia, isn't it?" Suddenly he looked us in the eye. When he knew that we knew what he feared, he treated us with compassion and concern. We knew the symptoms because the child of a friend of ours had died of leukemia. We knew.

We took our little girl to the hospital for tests, and she was so brave that her very gallantry brought tears to my eyes. We went home to our small apartment and sat in the big chair and told stories and knew that we would have several days' wait for the test results because of the holidays.

My husband was an actor. I am a writer. Like most artists, we had vivid imaginations. We tried hard not to project into the unknown future, to live right where we were, in a small apartment on 10th Street in New York City. We loved our apartment, where we slept on a couch in the living room. To get to the bedroom we had to walk through the kitchen and then the bathroom. At that time Leonard Bernstein lived on the top floor and would occasionally knock on our door to leave his suitcases when he did not want the long climb

41

up the stairs. We were happy. My husband was playing on Broadway. I had had two books published and was working on a third. We had a beautiful child.

And suddenly the foundations rocked beneath us. We understood tragedy and that no one is immune. We remembered a church in New England where, carved in the wood of the lintel, are the words: REMEMBER, NO IS AN ANSWER.

My mother grew up in a world of Bible stories, and I thought of the marvelous story of Shadrach, Meshach, and Abednego. These three young men refused to bow down to an idol, a golden image, and King Nebuchadnezzar was so furious that he ordered them to be thrown into a furnace so hot that the soldiers who threw them into the fire were killed by the heat.

But Shadrach, Meshach, and Abednego stood there in the flames, unhurt, and sang a song of praise of all creation.

King Nebuchadnezzar was astonished and asked, "Did we not cast three men bound into the fire?" They answered, "True, O King." He replied, "But I see four men loose, walking in the midst of the fire, and they are not hurt, and the appearance of the fourth is like the Son of God."

And that, perhaps, is the most astounding part of the whole story. God did not take Shadrach, Meshach, and Abednego out of the fiery furnace. God was in the flames with them.

Yes, it is a marvelous story, but I thought, *I am not Shadrach, Meshach, or Abednego and the flames burn.*

I rocked my child and told her stories and prayed incoherent prayers. We turned on the lights of the Christmas tree, lit a fire in our fireplace, turned out all the other lights, and I managed to sing lullabies without letting my voice break, or tears flow. When my husband got home from the theater we put her to bed, and we held each other. We knew that the promise has never been safety, or that bad things would not happen if we were good and virtuous. The promise is only that God is in it with us, no matter what it is.

Even before the test results came from the hospital our little girl began to revive, to laugh, to wriggle as we sat together on the piano bench to sing carols. Our hearts began to lift as we saw full life returning to her, and the tests when they were returned indicated that she had had an infection. It was not leukemia. She was going to be all right. She is now a beautiful young woman with children of her own, and she has gone through her own moments of terror when her eldest child was almost killed by a car. I suspect that most parents know these times. I know that the outcome is not always the one we pray for. In my own life there have been times when the answer has indeed been NO. My husband died, and I will miss him forever. This past July 28 the car I was in was hit by a truck and I was almost killed. I am still recuperating and wondering by what miracle my life was saved, and for what purpose. Certainly everything is more poignant. Were the autumn leaves this year more radiant than usual? What about the tiny new moon I saw last night? And my family and my friends: Have I ever loved them as much as I love them now?

I think back to that Christmas when my husband and I did not know whether our little girl would live to grow up.

Between that Christmas and this there have been many times when I have been in the fiery furnace, but I am beginning to understand who is in there with me and that when I need it, I am given courage I never knew I had. Every day is a miracle, and I hope that is something I will never forget.

Summer's End

Now the long golden shadows of evening no longer stretch across the field. Shadows already hover in the corners. Nevertheless we set the table for dinner outdoors. It is cool enough so that I put on my old polo coat. My feet in summer sandals are cool. Long before we finish eating we have to light the hurricane lamps. We sit there watching the last pale light leave the sky, the first stars tremble into the darkness. Then the Big Dipper is there, and Cassiopeia's Chair, brilliant against the night. Summer is over.

Calling, Calling

One foggy night I was walking the dogs down the lane and heard the geese, very close overhead, calling, calling, their marvellous strange cry, as they flew by. I think that is what our own best prayer must sound like when we send it up to heaven.

And indeed prayers continue and will continue. Mostly my prayers are almost wordless, just a holding out to God of your names, and then I can call on the Spirit, like the geese.

A Thanksgiving Weekend

Snow fell on Friday, a lovely clinging whiteness that outlined every twig and branch and blade of grass. Now we have had rain and the snow is all gone, but it was just right for a Thanksgiving weekend in the country.

A child's prayer

Thank you, God, for water,
for the water of the ocean
in which I paddle with my bare feet
and let the sand squish through my toes.
Thank you for the water from the brook
which flows even in the winter
under the ice.

That Tiny Flame

I think of James Clement (in *The Love Letters* and *Certain Women*) telling about the making of cider in the winter, when it is put outdoors to freeze. In the center of the frozen apple juice is a tiny core of pure flame that does not freeze. My faith (which I enjoy) is like that tiny flame. Even in the worst of moments it has been there, surrounded by ice, perhaps, but alive.

Crosswicks: An Old Pattern

I was grateful at Christmastide to have time for these thoughts, away from the busy schedule which never seems to let up in the city. Here, at night, I can listen to the silence which is broken not by sirens and taxi horns but by the creaking of a house that is about two hundred and fifty years old. It was built by hardy folk. They didn't have the machinery we have to make things easier. Men and mules did the work. The wood for our house didn't come from a lumberyard, but from the great forest that surrounded the original village; it must have taken incredible strength to have felled the tree that is our roof beam.

And those who built had to be hardy spiritually as well as physically. The doors at Crosswicks are Cross-and-Bible doors. The hardware is HL—Help Lord—and they needed help. The weak survived neither the long, cold winters nor the heat of summer. Women and infants died in childbirth; grief was a daily companion, but it was also part of their spiritual life, their pattern of creation.

The glory

Without any rhyme
without any reason
my heart lifts to light
in this bleak season

Believer and wanderer
caught by salvation
stumbler and blunderer
into Creation

In this cold blight
where marrow is frozen
it is God's time
my heart has chosen

In paradox and story
parable and laughter
find I the glory
here in hereafter

Into the darkest hour

It was a time like this,
War & tumult of war,
a horror in the air.
Hungry yawned the abyss—
and yet there came the star
and the child most wonderfully there.

It was a time like this
of fear & lust for power,
license & greed and blight—
and yet the Prince of bliss
came into the darkest hour
in quiet & silent light.

And in a time like this
how celebrate his birth
when all things fall apart?
Ah! wonderful it is
with no room on the earth
the stable is our heart.

An Open Window

If I look for an icon for Christmas, what I see is a mother and child and the radiant love between them—not necessarily Mary, the mother of God, but any one of us human mothers holding our babe in delight and joy.

This icon, too, alas, can be idol. When a mother manipulates, controls, abuses, ignores, dominates, sees her own motherhood as more important than the child she has birthed, idolatry is again rampant. But the icon can remain clear even when we make mistakes, as all mothers do, as even Mary surely did. She, being human, could not comprehend the dual nature of her son. She wanted him to turn water into wine, to reveal his divinity, even though he made it quite clear that the time was not ready. We mortal mothers far too often do not want our children to be human. We are human creatures, and with the best will in the world we do the wrong things. But as long as we remember that Creation, including our children, is God's, not ours, the icon of mother and child can be an open window.

The Eve of Epiphany

When I was a little girl in France I put out my shoes on the Eve of Epiphany. They were only ordinary shoes, not proper sabots, so I wasn't sure that they would be noticed by the three Wise Men; but in the morning one shoe held a new drawing pad, and the other a box of colored pencils. I like the idea of presents and feasting on Twelfth Night, so that Christmas can follow quietly on Advent. Christmas doesn't start until Christmas Eve, and then it can go on and on and the tree shines as brightly on Epiphany as on Christmas Day.

And there's more time to make things, which is one of the joys of Christmas. Our favorite presents are the homemade ones. Several years ago we decided that we were not going to be bullied by the post office or the Greeting Card Establishment into mailing our cards well before Christmas. We make our own cards, and I may not get an idea for one well before Christmas, for one thing. And there are a goodly number of people we write to only once a year, tucking the letter in with the card. So for the past several years we've taken our time, and as long as the last Christmas letter gets mailed before Lent, that's all I worry about, and Epiphany is a season of joy instead of exhaustion.

Epiphany
Unclench your fists
Hold out your hands.
Take mine.
Let us hold each other:
Thus is his Glory
Manifest.

God became man, was born of a woman, and we would have liked to keep this man-child with us forever; and that kind of possessiveness leads to disaster; as most parents know.

When I wrote the following lines I thought of them as being in Mary's voice, but they might just as well be in mine—or any parent's.

Now we may love the child.
Now he is ours,
this tiny thing,

utterly vulnerable and dependent
on the circle of our love.
Now we may hold him,
feeling with gentle hands
the perfection of his tender skin
from the soft crown of his head
to the sweet soles of his merrily kicking feet.
His fingers softly curl
around one finger of the grownup hand.
Now we may hold.
Now may I feel his hungry sucking at my breast
as I give him my own life.
Now may my husband toss him in the air
and catch him in his sure and steady hands
laughing with laughter as quick and pure
as the baby's own.
Now may I rock him softly to his sleep,
rock and sing,
sing and hold,
This moment of time is here,
has happened, is:
rejoice!

Child,
give me the courage
for the time
when I must open my arms
and let you go.

I looked at my last baby lying in his cradle, knowing that he was
the last child I would bear, for I nearly didn't survive his birth;
looked, touched, listened, with an incredible awareness I might not
have had if I had been able to expect to bear more children. As
each change came, I had to let the infant-that-was go, go forever.
When he was seven months old I weaned him, as part of that es-
sential letting go, letting him move on to child, little boy, young
man . . . Love, and let go. Love, and let go.

An Offering of Love

Jesus should be for us the icon of icons, God sending heaven to earth, "Lord of Lords in human vesture." God has given us each other as revelations of divine creativity, and the ultimate revelation is in Jesus of Nazareth, the Incarnation of God into human flesh: *carne* = flesh. God enfleshed for our sakes. God's love offered to us fully and wonderfully and particularly in one person.

Making worlds: a child's prayer

> Lord God,
> you took great big handfuls of
> chaos and made galaxies
> and stars and solar systems
> and night and day and sun and rain and snow
> and me.
> I take paint and crayon and paper
> and make worlds, too,
> along with you.

The Light of the Stars

One time, when I was little more than a baby, I was taken to visit my grandmother, who was living in a cottage on a nearly un-inhabited stretch of beach in northern Florida. All I remember of this visit is being picked up from my crib in what seemed the middle of the night and carried from my bedroom and out of doors, where I had my first look at the stars.

It must have been an unusually clear and beautiful night for some-one to have said, "Let's wake the baby and show her the stars." The night sky, the constant rolling of breakers against the shore, the stu-pendous light of the stars—all made an indelible impression on me. I was intuitively aware not only of a beauty I had never seen before but also that the world was far greater than the protected limits of the small child's world which was all that I had known thus far. I had a total, if not very conscious, moment of revelation; I saw crea-tion bursting the bounds of daily restriction, and stretching out from dimension to dimension, beyond any human comprehension.

This early experience was freeing, rather than daunting, and since it was the first, it has been the foundation for all other such glimpses of glory. And it is probably why the sound of the ocean and the sight of the stars give me more healing, more whole-ing, than any-thing else.

I turn again to the night sky, this time to a planet, one of the planets in our own solar system, the planet Mercury. Mercury re-volves around our mutual parent sun in such a way that one face is always turned toward the sun and is brilliantly lit and burningly hot; and the other side is always turned toward the cold dark of inter-stellar space. But Mercury oscillates slightly on its axis, and thereby sunside and nightside are integrated by a temperate zone which knows both heat and cold, light and dark. So the two disparate sides of Mercury are not separated by a chasm; the temperate zone me-diates.

Where, in ourselves, can we find this temperate zone which will integrate and free us? The words *freedom* and *liberation* have been used frequently during the last decade, and this would certainly seem to imply that we are less free, less liberated, than we want to admit. People who are already free don't need to talk about liberation. It is a great mistake to equate freedom with anarchy, liberation with chaos. It has been my experience that freedom comes as the tem-perate zone integrates sunside and nightside, thereby making whole-ness instead of brokenness.

An Icon of Creation

Stars have always been an icon of creation for me. During my high school years, when I was at my grandmother's beach cottage for vacations, I loved to lie on a sand dune and watch the stars come out over the ocean, often focusing on the brilliant grace of one particular star. Back in school, I wrote these lines:

> I gaze upon the steady star
> That comes from where I cannot see,
> And something from that distant far
>
> Pierces the waiting core of me
> And fills me with an aweful pain
> That I must count not loss but gain.
>
> If something from infinity
> Can touch and strike my very soul,
> Does that which comes from out of me
> Reach and pierce its far off goal?

Very young verses, but they contain the germ of an understanding of the interdependence of all Creation.

A Deepening Vision

During those weeks in Chamonix we went everywhere on skis, the simplest method of moving on the snow-packed streets, and I learned more complex skiing on the slopes above the villa. We spent a memorable day on the Mer de Glace, and those hours of walking over a sea of ice were a revelation of a cold and unearthly beauty I had never before seen. My own vision was deepened because I saw the beauty through the eyes of my parents; their wholehearted response took us all beyond the pain and confusion which were ever present in the villa. One night we rode for an hour in a horse-drawn sleigh, snow beneath us, moonlight and starlight above us, the horse's mane streaming coldly in the wind, while we were kept warm under fur robes. Father hardly coughed at all; Mother relaxed and enjoyed the beauty and the speed. I moved back into my dream world during that ride, not as an escape, but as a respite; I did not try to take the fairy tale with me back into the villa.

Revealing Structure

Strangely I have found in my own life that it is only through a wintry spirituality that I am able to affirm summer and sunshine. A friend wrote me recently, "Winter reveals structure." Only as the structure is firmly there are we able to dress it with the lovely trappings of spring, budding leaves, rosy blossoms. Winter is the quiet, fallow time when the earth prepares for the rebirth of spring. Unless the seed is put into the ground to die, it cannot be born.

A Promise of Spring

It's cold and clear, but there's a promise of spring as I look out the window and down the street where the trees in Riverside Park are faintly blurred against the sky as they are losing their winter starkness and are preparing to bud. I'm ready for new green and warmer breezes. Bion tells me that at Crosswicks the green shoots of daffodils have pushed up through the snow.

"Anesthetics"

Our youngest child, when he first became conscious of vocabulary, often did violence to words in absurd little ways which delighted us. Hugh and I listened seriously, lest we make him self-conscious or think we were laughing at him. We needn't have worried; he plunged into vocabulary like a seagull into water, entirely fascinated with whatever he came up with. Even the laughter of his elder siblings did not deter him, and he is now happily malapropping in Latin, French, and German. One day, aged seven, he came home from school highly indignant because the boys' gym period had been curtailed. "We only had ten minutes of gym," he said, "and that was all anesthetics."

This was not just something to laugh at; it sent me back to my own, dreaded gym periods where anesthetics rather than calisthenics would have been more than welcome. Any team I was on lost automatically; when teams were chosen, mine was the last name to be reluctantly called out, and the team which had the bad luck to get me let out uninhibited groans. I now have this emotion at my fingertips if I need it for a story I'm writing; or if I need it to comfort some child who is going through a similar experience. It does us good to listen to things differently.

I remember "anesthetics" not only because it reminded me of my own pains over gym but because this small, delectable laugh came while I was in the middle of a very bad period, literarily speaking, and needed any reason for laughter, no matter how trivial. *A Wrinkle in Time* was on its long search for a publisher. Finally one, who had kept the manuscript for three months, turned it down on the Monday before Christmas. I remember sitting on the foot of our bed, tying up Christmas presents, and feeling cold and numb: anesthetized. I was congratulating myself on being controlled and grown-up, and found out only later that I'd made a mess of the Christmas presents; I'd sent some heady perfume to a confirmed bachelor, and a sober necktie to a sixteen-year-old girl. So I called Theron, my agent: "Send the manuscript back to me. Nobody's ever going to take it, it's too peculiar, and it just isn't fair to the family." He didn't want to send it back, but I was cold and stubborn, and finally he gave in.

My mother was with us for the holidays, and shortly after Christmas I had a small party for her with some of her old friends. One of them, Hester Stover, more than ever dear to me now, said,

"Madeleine, you must meet my friend, John Farrar." I made some kind of disgruntled noise, because I never wanted to see another publisher; I was back to thinking I ought to learn to bake cherry pie. But Hester, going to a good deal of trouble, insisted on setting up an appointment, and I took the subway down to John Farrar's office. I just happened to have that rather bulky manuscript under my arm.

He couldn't have been kinder or warmer. He knew some of my other work and was generous enough to say that he liked it, and he asked me what I was up to now. I explained that I had a book that I kind of liked, but nobody else did, or if they did, they were afraid of it.

I left it with him. Within two weeks I was having lunch with him and Hal Vursell, and signing a contract. "But don't be disappointed if it doesn't do well," they told me. "We're publishing it because we love it."

It is a right and proper Cinderella story. And I'm sure Cinderella appreciated her ball gown more because she'd been forced to sit by the ashes in rags for a long time before her fairy godmother arrived.

One king's epiphany

I shall miss the stars.

Not that I shall stop looking
as they pattern their wild wills each night
across an inchoate sky, but I must see them with a different awe.
If I trace their flames' ascending and descending—
relationships and correspondences—
then I deny what they have just revealed.
The sum of their oppositions, juxtapositions,
led me to the end of all sums:
a long journey, cold, dark, and uncertain,
toward the ultimate equation.
How can I understand? If I turn back from this,
compelled to seek all answers in the stars,
then this—Who—they have led me to
is not the One they said: they will have lied.
No stars are liars!
My life on their truth!
If they had lied about this
I could never trust their power again.

But I believe they showed the truth,
truth breathing,
truth Whom I have touched with my own hands,
worshipped with my gifts.
If I have bowed, made
obeisance to this final arithmetic,
I cannot ask the future from the stars without betraying
the One whom they have led me to.
It will be hard not to ask, just once again,
to see by mathematical forecast where he will grow,
where go, what kingdom conquer, what crown wear.
But would it not be going beyond truth
(the obscene *reductio ad absurdum*)
to lose my faith in truth once, and once for all
revealed in the full dayspring of the sun?
I cannot go back to night.
O Truth, O small and unexpected thing,
You have taken so much from me.
How can I bear wisdom's pain?
But I have been shown: and I have seen.

Yes. I shall miss the stars.

Glorious Mystery

Who is that tiny baby? Even the Creator, almighty and terrible and incomprehensible! . . . Whose arms encircled the world with . . . grace.

—from "Falling into Sentimentality" and "Mary speaks"

The ordinary so extraordinary

He came, quietly impossible,
Out of a young girl's womb,
A love as amazingly marvelous
As his bursting from the tomb.

This child was fully human,
This child was wholly God.
The hands of All Love fashioned him
Of mortal flesh and bone and blood,

The ordinary so extraordinary
The stars shook in the sky
As the Lord of all the universe
Was born to live, to love, to die.

He came, quietly impossible:
Nothing will ever be the same:
Jesus, the Light of every heart—
The God we know by Name.

The Glorious Mystery

Rise up, with willing feet
Go forth, the Bridegroom meet:
Alleluia!
Bear through the night
Your well-trimmed light,
Speed forth to join the marriage rite.

All hail, Incarnate Lord,
Our crown, and our reward!
Alleluia!
We haste along,
In pomp of song,
And gladsome join the marriage throng.

Lamb of God, the heav'ns adore thee,
And men and angels sing before thee,
With harp and cymbal's clearest tone.
By the pearly gates in wonder
We stand, and swell the voice of thunder
That echoes round thy dazzling throne.
No vision ever brought,
No ear hath ever caught
Such rejoicing:
We raise the song, We swell the throng,
*To praise thee ages all along. Amen.**

Wachet Auf (Sleepers, Wake) by Philip Nicolai; translated by Catherine Winkworth.

You shall know him when he comes
Not by any din of drums
Nor by the vantage of His airs
Nor by anything he wears—
Neither by his crown—
Nor his gown—
For his Presence known shall be
By the Holy Harmony
*That His coming makes in thee.**

W ho was he, this tiny babe whose birth we celebrate at Christmas time, whose Resurrection lightens our hearts at Easter, and whose coming in glory we await?

He was born, as we are all born, of water and blood, of a human mother, a young girl whose courage is awesome. It was a difficult birth in those days when often women and infants did not survive childbirth. Mary was not able to have her baby at home. Her mother was not able to be with her, to comfort her. There was no trained midwife or doctor. She lived in a small country, an outpost in the Roman Empire, and when Rome declared a census, there was no excuse: Mary and Joseph were required to go to Bethlehem and register, because Joseph was *of the house of David.*

The closest we can come to understanding what it is like to be controlled by an alien power is to think of Poland or France under Nazi domination; of countries such as Albania, taken over by the Soviet Union. The ordinary people, living and working and loving and birthing, don't get consulted on these matters.

Mary and Joseph were just such ordinary people. Joseph was a carpenter, and solidly middle class. And when Rome said, "Come and be counted," they had no choice.

And so, as the Gospel of Luke tells us, it was while they were in Bethlehem, that the time came for Mary to deliver. *And she brought forth her firstborn son, and wrapped him in swaddling clothes, and laid him in a manger, because there was no room for them in the inn.*

The manger was likely in a cave in the hills, rather than in the kind of barn we see today. When I was in Jerusalem, I saw similar caves for domestic animals, built into the hillside, and outlined with the golden stones of that blue and gold land.

*Unknown 15th century writer.

Of the Father's love begotten,
Ere the worlds began to be,
He is Alpha and Omega,
    He the source, the ending he,
Of the things that are, that have been,
    And that future years shall see,
    Evermore and evermore!

O that birth forever blessed,
    When the Virgin, full of grace,
By the Holy Ghost conceiving,
    Bore the Saviour of our race;
And the Babe, the world's Redeemer,
    First revealed his sacred face,
    Evermore and evermore!

O ye heights of heav'n adore him;
    Angel hosts, his praises sing;
Powers, dominions, bow before him,
    And extol our God and King;
Let no tongue on earth be silent,
    Every voice in concert ring,
    Evermore and evermore!

Thee let old men, thee let young men,
    Thee let boys in chorus sing;
Matrons, virgins, little maidens,
    With glad voices answering:
Let their guileless songs re-echo,
    And the heart its music bring,
    Evermore and evermore!

Christ, to thee with God the Father,
    And, O Holy Ghost, to thee,
Hymn and chant and high thanksgiving,
    And unwearied praises be:
Honor, glory, and dominion,
    And eternal victory,
    Evermore and evermore!*

*By Marcus Aurelius Clemens Prudentius; translated by John Mason Neale, Henry Williams Baker.

This ancient hymn, written in the early centuries of Christendom, makes it very clear that Christ always was. He didn't suddenly appear in a manger in Bethlehem two thousand years ago. He was. He is. He will be. This total *is*ness is more than our finite minds can readily understand. It is nothing that can be comprehended in the language of literal thinking. But in his Gospel, Matthew quotes Jesus as saying, *I thank you, O Father, Lord of heaven and earth, because you have hidden these things from the wise and prudent, and have revealed them to children.*

If we turn away from the child, the poet, the artist in ourselves, we lose the ability to believe the glorious mysteries that lift us from being nothing more than a few nearly valueless molecules to children of light, creatures called to create along with our Creator.

So we rejoice in the mystery of this tiny baby. We give presents to each other as reminders of his great gift of himself to us. We trim the Christmas tree, although the Christmas tree was not originally a Christian symbol, but came out of northern Europe and the worship of different gods. But any affirmation of love and beauty can become Christian, because Christianity is totally committed to incarnation. The decorated tree may have secular origins, but if we truly believe in incarnation, then everything secular can also be sacred. So we trim our trees and make them sparkle with light as a symbol that light is stronger than darkness, and even in a world as dark as ours, the light still shines, and cannot be extinguished.

> This is no time for a child to be born,
> With the Earth betrayed by war and hate
> And a comet slashing the sky to warn
> That time runs out and the sun burns late.
>
> That was no time for a child to be born
> In a land in the crushing grip of Rome;
> Honor and truth were trampled by scorn—
> Yet here did the Saviour make his home.
>
> When is the time for love to be born?
> The inn is full on planet earth,
> And by a comet the sky is torn—
> Yet Love still takes the risk of birth.

This tiny baby

Whoever is the baby?
Nothing but a little lamb
who says God is and that I am.

Who is this tiny baby?
Just an infant, meek and mild,
just a feeble, mortal child.

Who is this tiny baby?
The Lord strong and mighty
even the Lord mighty in battle.

The king of glory's coming
who is this
even the Lord of Hosts
This is the tiny baby!

Falling into Sentimentality

I love the Christmas tree with the family gathering together to decorate it, but I wish that we were like the French (and many others) who do their gift-giving on Epiphany, with the coming of the Wise Men, and keep Christmas Day itself as a holy day. We forget the holiness and fall into sentimentality over the tiny baby in the stable. Who is that tiny baby? Even the Creator, almighty and terrible and incomprehensible!

January: With My Own Eyes

New Year's Eve and New Year's Day come not out of the church year but out of the dawn of human life. To our ancient forbears, many thousands of years before the birth of Jesus, the stretching nights of early winter and the shortening days were terrifying. Was the night going to swallow up the day? Was the life-giving sun going to slide down the western horizon and be lost forever? It must have seemed a real possibility to those dwellers in caves or tree houses, who knew nothing they could not see with their own eyes about the movements of the suns and the stars.

So, when it slowly became apparent that the sun was staying in the sky a minute longer than it had the day before, and then a minute longer, there was great rejoicing, and feasting and fun, and very likely (as today) too much fun. But it was more than fun. It was spontaneous gratitude that the world was not coming to an end.

In the story of the life of Jesus, the first day of January is marked as the feast of his circumcision. All good Jewish boys were ritually circumcised in the first ten days of their lives. So Joseph and Mary carried the eight-day-old baby to the temple and made the required offerings, *according to that which is said in the law of the Lord, a pair of turtle-doves or two young pigeons.* You might have thought that they would have had family and friends with them for this great event, but even in babyhood it seemed that Jesus turned things upside down. As far as we know there were only three witnesses: the high priest, a very old man named Simeon, and an equally old woman named Anna. Simeon believed that he would not die until he had seen the promised Messiah, and when the baby was put in his arms, he said words which for centuries have been part of evening prayer:

> *Lord, now let your servant depart in peace as you have promised,*
> *For with my own eyes I have seen the Saviour*
> *which you prepared in the sight of all people*
> *To be a light to give light to the Gentiles,*
> *and to be the glory of your people, Israel.*

An old man and an old woman were the first to acknowledge that this baby was the one they had spent their lives hoping for, the Saviour that all Jews hoped for. Simeon, after his own joyous recognition of the infant, promised Mary nothing easy; a sword would go through her own heart, he prophesied. And Mary must have turned cold inwardly.

But she was young enough to be able to accept difficult demands with courage, and to know that the way of the world is not always the way of the Lord.

The Lord is King, and hath put on glorious apparel;
The Lord hath put on his apparel,
And girded himself with strength.
But not the kind of glorious apparel or worldly power that might
have been expected.

Like every newborn, he has come from very far.
His eyes are blinded by the brilliance of the star.
So glorious is he, he goes to this immoderate length
To show his love for us, discarding power and strength.
Girded for war, humility his mighty dress,
He moves into the battle wholly weaponless.

We don't know much about Jesus' early life. It's likely his father
taught him carpentry, and this would have developed his muscles
and helped to make him a strong man. His mother must have mar-
velled at him, wondered about the angel who came to her to an-
nounce his birth, and then the birth itself, with the shepherds
coming to bring their humble gifts, and the kings their magnificent
ones.

O Simplicitas

An angel came to me
and I was unprepared
to be what God was using.
Mother I was to be.
A moment I despaired,
thought briefly of refusing.
The angel knew I heard.
According to God's Word
I bowed to this strange choosing.

A palace should have been
the birthplace of a king
(I had no way of knowing).
We went to Bethlehem;
it was so strange a thing.
The wind was cold, and blowing,
my cloak was old, and thin.
They turned us from the inn;
the town was overflowing.

God's Word, a child so small
who still must learn to speak
lay in humiliation.
Joseph stood, strong and tall.
The beasts were warm and meek
and moved with hesitation.
The Child born in a stall?
I understood it: all.
Kings came in adoration.

Perhaps it was absurd;
a stable set apart,
the sleepy cattle lowing;
and the incarnate Word
resting against my heart.
My joy was overflowing.
The shepherds came, adored
the folly of the Lord,
wiser than all men's knowing.

The promise of his birth

In the beginning I was confused and dazzled,
a plain girl, unused to talking with angels.
Then there was the hard journey to Bethlehem,
and the desperate search for a place to stay,
my distended belly ripe and ready for deliverance.
In the dark of the cave, night air sweet with the moist breath
of the domestic beasts, I laughed, despite my pains,
at their concern. Joseph feared that they would frighten me
with their anxious stampings and snortings,
but their fear was only for me, and not because of me.
One old cow, udders permanently drooping,
lowed so with my every contraction
that my own birthing cries could not be heard,
and so my baby came with pain and tears and much hilarity.

Afterwards, swaddled and clean, he was so small and tender
that I could not think beyond my present loving
to all this strange night pointed. The shepherds came,
clumsy and gruff, and knelt and bought their gifts,
and, later on, the Kings; and all I knew was marvel.
His childhood was sheer joy to me. He was merry and loving,
moved swiftly from laughters to long, unchildlike silences.
The years before his death were bitter to taste.
I did not understand, and sometimes thought that it was he
who had lost sight of the promise of his birth.

Mary speaks

O you who bear the pain of the whole earth,
    I bore you.
O you whose tears give human tears their worth,
    I laughed with you.
You, who, when your hem is touched, give power,
    I nourished you.
Who turn the day to night in this dark hour,
    light comes from you.
O you who hold the world in your embrace,
    I carried you.
Whose arms encircled the world with your grace,
    I once held you.
O you who laughed and ate and walked the shore,
    I played with you.
And I, who with all others, you died for,
    now I hold you.

May I be faithful to this final test:
in this last time I hold my child, my son,
his body close enfolded to my breast,
the holder held: the bearer borne.
Mourning to joy: darkness to morn.
Open, my arms: your work is done.

More Than We Can Do

We are all asked to do more than we can do. Every hero and heroine of the Bible does more than he would have thought it possible to do, from Gideon to Esther to Mary.

The Furthest Reaches of Time and Space

My apartment faces west, and when I go to bed at night and turn out the lights I can see across the great Hudson River to the lights of New Jersey. I can often see the planes coming in, en route to La Guardia Airport, looking like moving stars, though even when the sky is clear there are few real stars visible because of the city lights that burn all night. I think of the nearest star, Proxima Centauri, about four light years away—about twenty-three million million miles. The rare stars I see may be three hundred light years away, and three thousand light years away, and three million. When we human creatures look up at the night sky we are able to see into the furthest reaches of time.

Not only time, but space—vast distances. Galaxies trillions of light years across. Suns so enormous that they make our own sun a mere pinprick.

Atomic Furnaces

The morning star is low on the horizon. There are three more stars pulsing faintly in the city sky. But even if I can't see a skyful of stars they are there above me nevertheless; the Milky Way, our own galaxy, swings somewhere in the vast dark above the city lights.

All those stars. Suns. More suns than can be imagined. Great flaming brilliant atomic furnaces, the bursting of their atoms providing life. Providing life for their planets. Perhaps there are planets where that which was created by love returns love, and there is joy and worship and praise, and man sings with the angels.

Soaring

When I think of the incredible, incomprehensible sweep of creation above me, I have the strange reaction of feeling fully alive. Rather than feeling lost and unimportant and meaningless, set against galaxies which go beyond the reach of the furthest telescopes, I feel that my life has meaning. Perhaps I should feel insignificant, but instead I feel a soaring in my heart that the God who could create all this—and out of nothing—can still count the hairs of my head.

Wonderful Mix of Creation

Christ, the second Person of the Trinity, has always been, is always, and always will be available to all people and at all times. We are so focused on the Incarnation, on Jesus of Nazareth, that sometimes we forget that the Second Person of the Trinity didn't just arrive two thousand years ago, but has always been. Christ was the Word that shouted all of Creation into being, all the galaxies and solar systems, all the subatomic particles, and the wonderful mix of Creation that is what makes up each one of us.

Jesus said, to the horror of the establishment people, "Before Abraham was, I am."

This Extraordinary Birth

The Nativity is a time to take courage. How brave am I? Can I bear, without breaking apart, this extraordinary birth?

After annunciation

This is the irrational season
When love blooms bright and wild.
Had Mary been filled with reason
There'd have been no room for the child.

The Bethlehem explosion

And it came to pass in those days, that there went out a decree from Caesar Augustus, that all the world should be taxed. . . . And Joseph also went up from Galilee . . . to be taxed with Mary his espoused wife, being great with child.—Gospel of Luke

The chemistry lab at school
was in an old greenhouse
surrounded by ancient live oaks
garnished with Spanish moss.

The experiment I remember best
was pouring a quart of clear fluid
into a glass jar, and dropping into it,
grain by grain, salt-sized crystals,
until they layered
like white sand on the floor of the jar.

One more grain—and suddenly—
water and crystal burst
into a living, moving pattern,
a silent, quietly violent explosion.
The teacher told us that only when
we supersaturated the solution,
would come the precipitation.

The little town
was like the glass jar in our lab.
One by one they came, grain by grain,
all those of the house of David,
like grains of sand to be counted.

The inn was full. When Joseph knocked,
his wife was already in labour; there was no room
even for compassion. Until the barn was offered.
That was the precipitating factor. A child was born,
and the pattern changed forever, the cosmos
shaken with that silent explosion.

The Other Side of Reason

To paint a picture or to write a story or to compose a song is an incarnational activity. The artist is a servant who is willing to be a birthgiver. In a very real sense the artist (male or female) should be like Mary, who, when the angel told her that she was to bear the Messiah, was obedient to the command.

Obedience is an unpopular word nowadays, but the artist must be obedient to the work, whether it be a symphony, a painting, or a story for a small child. I believe that each work of art, whether it is a work of great genius, or something very small, comes to the artist and says, "Here I am. Enflesh me. Give birth to me." And the artist either says, "My soul doth magnify the Lord," and willingly becomes the bearer of the work, or refuses; but the obedient response is not necessarily a conscious one, and not everyone has the humble, courageous obedience of Mary.

As for Mary, she was little more than a child when the angel came to her; she had not lost her child's creative acceptance of the realities moving on the other side of the everyday world. We lose our ability to see angels as we grow older, and that is a tragic loss.

God, through the angel Gabriel, called on Mary to do what, in the world's eyes, is impossible, and instead of saying, "I can't," she replied immediately, "Be it unto me according to thy Word."

How difficult we find the Annunciation. How could one young, untried girl contain within her womb the power which created the galaxies? How could that power be found in the helplessness of an infant? It is more than we, in our limited, literal-mindedness, can cope with, and so we hear, "I can't be a Christian because I can't believe in the virgin birth," as though faith were something which lay within the realm of verification. If it can be verified, we don't need faith.

I don't need faith to know that if a poem has fourteen lines, a specific rhyme scheme, and is in iambic pentameter, it is a sonnet; it may not be a good sonnet, but it will be a sonnet. I don't need faith to know that if I take flour and butter and milk and seasonings and heat them in a double boiler, the mix will thicken and become white sauce. Faith is for that which lies on the other side of reason. Faith is what makes life bearable, with all its tragedies and ambiguities and sudden, startling joys. Surely it wasn't reasonable of the Lord of the Universe to come down and walk this earth with us and love us enough to die for us and then show us everlasting life? We will all grow old, and sooner or later we will die, like the old trees in the orchard. But we have been promised that this is not the end. We have been promised life.

What would have happened to Mary (and to all the rest of us) if she had said No to the angel? She was free to do so. But she said Yes. She was obedient, and the artist, too, must be obedient to the command of the work, knowing that this involves long hours of research, of throwing out a month's work, of going back to the beginning, or, sometimes, scrapping the whole thing. The artist, like Mary, is free to say No. When a shoddy novel is published, the writer is rejecting the obedient response, taking the easy way out. But when the words mean even more than the writer knew they meant, then the writer has been listening. And sometimes when we listen, we are led into places we do not expect, into adventures we do not always understand.

Mary did not always understand. But one does not have to understand to be obedient. Instead of understanding—that intellectual understanding which we are so fond of—there is a feeling of rightness, of knowing, knowing things which we are not yet able to understand.

A young woman said to me, during the question-and-answer period after a lecture, "I read *A Wrinkle in Time* when I was eight or nine. I didn't understand it, but I knew what it was about."

As long as we know what it's about, then we can have the courage to go wherever we are asked to go, even if we fear that the road may take us through danger and pain.

The birth of wonder

When I am able to pray with the mind in the heart, I am joyfully able to affirm the irrationality of Christmas.

As I grow older
I get surer
Man's heart is colder,
His life no purer.
As I grow steadily
More austere
I come less readily
To Christmas each year.
I can't keep taking
Without a thought
Forced merrymaking
And presents bought
In crowds and jostling.
Alas, there's naught
In empty wassailing
Where oblivion's sought.
Oh, I'd be waiting
With quiet fasting
Anticipating
A joy more lasting.
And so I rhyme
With no apology
During this time
Of eschatology:
Judgment and warning
Come like thunder.
But now is the hour
When I remember
An infant's power
On a cold December.
Midnight is dawning
And the birth of wonder.

Redemption

He did not wait . . .

till hearts were pure. In joy he came

to a tarnished world of sin and doubt.

To a world like ours, of anguished shame

he came, and his Light would not go out.

—from "First coming"

The First-born light

The Maker's hand flung stars across the night
with angels bursting forth from galaxies
new music singing from the spheres in harmonies
that blessed the dancing of the first-born light.

And then the light was darkened by an earth
dimmed by torn dreams, saddened by shrill pride.
Stars faded, lost their story, and died.
The dance distorted in strange lies and anger.
Love's hand again was lifted. In a manger
Again the Maker of the stars gave birth.

The Wise Men

A star has streaked the sky,
pulls us,
calls.
Where, oh where, where leads the light?

We came and left our gifts
and turned
homeward.
Time had passed, friends gone from sight—

One by one, they go, they die
to now,
to us—
gone in the dazzling dark of night.

Oh how, and where, and when, and why,
and what,
and who,
and may, and should, O God, and might

a star, a wind, a laugh, a cry
still come
from one—
the blazing word of power and might—

to use our gifts of gold and myrrh
and frankincense
as needed,
as our intention was to do the right?

Here, there, hear—soft as a sigh—
willing,
loving
all that is spoken, back to the flight

blazing too fierce for mortal eye.
Renew—
redeem,
oh, Love, until we, too, may dazzle bright.

Annunciation

1

Sorrowfully
the angel appeared
before the young woman
feared
to ask what must be asked,
a task
almost too great to bear.
With care,
mournfully,
the angel bare
the tidings of great joy,
and then
great grief.
Behold, thou shalt conceive.
Thou shalt bring forth a son.
This must be done.
There will be no reprieve.

2

Another boy
born of woman (who shall also grieve)
full of grace
and innocence
and no offence—
a lovely one
of pure and unmarked face.

3

How much can a woman bear?

4

Pain will endure for a night
but joy comes in the morning.

His name is Judas.

That the prophets may be fulfilled
he must play his part.
It must be done.
Pain will endure.
Joy comes in the morning.

Opposing Parallels: A Journal Entry

A group of us from Regent and Vancouver School of Theology went to an excellent production of *Much Ado About Nothing* at Bard on the Beach. I've always loved the play because of Beatrice and Benedick, Beatrice being one of the best, funniest, and warmest of Shakespeare's women's roles.

Hero, Beatrice's cousin, and Claudio come off much less well. Hero is set up by the villain to look as though she is being unfaithful to her fiancé on the eve of their wedding. Claudio believes the cruel hoax without question and then, with vicious cruelty, allows the wedding to take place as planned until the moment when the friar asks if anyone knows of any impediment, at which point he brutally and publicly denounces the innocent Hero.

It reminded me of another man whose fiancé seems to have betrayed him at the last minute. Instead of denouncing her, having her stoned—the customary punishment for adultery—he lovingly decides to send her away to some safe place.

And then he is willing to believe the angel who tells him not to be afraid to take the young girl for his wife, for the child within her is from God.

I wonder if Shakespeare was aware of the opposing parallels?

Bearer of love

The great swan's wings were wild as he flew down;
Leda was almost smothered in his embrace.
His crimson beak slashed fiercely at her gown—
lust deepened by the terror on her face.

Semele saw her lover as a god.
Her rash desire was blatant, undenied.
He showed himself, thunder and lightning shod.
Her human eyes were blasted and she died.

And Mary sat, unknowing, unaware.
The angel's wings were wilder than the swan
as God broke through the shining, waiting air,
gave her the lily's sword thrust and was gone.

The swans, the old gods fall in consternation
at the fierce coming of the wild wind's thrust
entering Mary in pure penetration.
The old gods die now, crumbled stone and rust.

Young Mary, moved by Gabriel, acquiesced,
asked nothing for herself in lowliness,
accepted, too, the pain, and then, most blest,
became the bearer of all holiness.

O Sapientia

It was from Joseph first I learned
of love. Like me he was dismayed.
How easily he could have turned
me from his house; but, unafraid,
he put me not away from him
(O God-sent angel, pray for him).
Thus through his love was Love obeyed.
The Child's first cry came like a bell:
God's Word aloud, God's Word in deed.
The angel spoke: so it befell,
and Joseph with me in my need.
O Child whose father came from heaven,
to you another gift was given,
your earthly father chosen well.

With Joseph I was always warmed
and cherished. Even in the stable
I knew that I would not be harmed.
And, though above the angels swarmed,
man's love it was that made me able
to bear God's love, wild, formidable,
to bear God's will, through me performed.

A Time of Hope

Cribb'd, cabined, and confined within the contours of a human infant. The infinite defined by the finite? The Creator of all life thirsty and abandoned? Why would he do such a thing? Aren't there easier and better ways for God to redeem his fallen creatures?

And what good did it all do? The heart of man is still evil. Wars grow more terrible with each generation. The earth daily becomes more depleted by human greed. God came to save us and we thank him by producing bigger and better battlefields and slums and insane asylums.

And yet Christmas is still for me a time of hope, of hope for the courage to love and accept love, a time when I can forget that my Christology is extremely shaky and can rejoice in God's love through love of family and friends.

A Full House: An Austin Family Story

To anybody who lives in a city or even a sizable town, it may not sound like much to be the director of a volunteer choir in a postcard church in a postcard village, but I was the choir director and largely responsible for the Christmas Eve service, so it was very much of a much for me. I settled my four children and my father, who was with us for Christmas, in a front pew and went up to the stuffy choir-robing room. I was missing my best baritone, my husband, Wally, because he had been called to the hospital. He's a country doctor, and I'm used to his pocket beeper going off during the church service. I missed him, of course, but I knew he'd been called to deliver a baby, and a Christmas baby is always a joy.

The service went beautifully. Nobody flatted, and Eugenia Underhill, my lead soprano, managed for once not to breathe in the middle of a word. The only near disaster came when she reached for the high C in *O Holy Night*, hit it brilliantly––and then down fell her upper plate. Eugenia took it in good stride, pushed her teeth back in place and finished her solo. When she sat down, she doubled over with mirth.

The church looked lovely, lighted entirely by candlelight, with pine boughs and holly banking the windows. The Christmas Eve service is almost entirely music, hence my concern; there is never a sermon, but our minister reads excerpts from the Christmas sermons of John Donne and Martin Luther.

When the dismissal and blessing were over, I heaved a sigh of relief. Now I could attend to our own Christmas at home. I collected my family, and we went out into the night. A soft, feathery snow was beginning to fall. People called out "Good-night" and "Merry Christmas." I was happily tired, and ready for some peace and quiet for the rest of the evening—our service is over by nine.

I hitched Rob, my sleeping youngest, from one hip to the other. The two girls, Vicky and Suzy, walked on either side of their grandfather; John, my eldest, was with me. They had all promised to go to bed without protest as soon as we had finished all our traditional Christmas rituals. We seem to add new ones each year, so the Christmas-Eve bedtime gets later and later.

I piled the kids into the station wagon, thrusting Rob into John's arms. Father and I got in the front, and I drove off into the snow, which was falling more heavily. I hoped that it would not be a blizzard and that Wally would get home before the roads got too bad.

Our house is on the crest of a hill, a mile out of the village. As I looked uphill, I could see the lights of our outdoor Christmas tree twinkling warmly through the snow. I turned up our back road, feeling suddenly very tired. When I drove up to the garage and saw that Wally's car was not there, I tried not to let Father or the children see my disappointment. I began ejecting the kids from the back. It was my father who first noticed what looked like a bundle of clothes by the storm door.

"Victoria," he called to me. "What's this?"

The bundle of clothes moved. A tear-stained face emerged, and I recognized Evie, who had moved from the village with her parents two years ago, when she was sixteen. She had been our favorite and most loyal baby-sitter, and we all missed her. I hadn't seen her—or heard anything about her—in all this time.

"Evie!" I cried. "What is it? What's the matter?"

She moved stiffly, as though she had been huddled there in the cold for a long time. Then she held her arms out to me in a childlike gesture. "Mrs. Austin—" She sighed as I bent down to kiss her. And then, "Mom threw me out. So I came here." She dropped the words simply, as though she had no doubt that she would find a welcome in our home. She had on a shapeless, inadequate coat, and a bare toe stuck through a hole in one of her sneakers.

I put my arms around her and helped her up. "Come in. You must be frozen."

The children were delighted to see Evie and crowded around, hugging her, so it was a few minutes before we got into the kitchen and past the dogs who were loudly welcoming us home. There were Mr. Rochester, our Great Dane; Colette, a silver-gray French Poodle who bossed the big dog unmercifully; and, visiting us for the Christmas holidays while his owners were on vacation, a ten-month-old Manchester terrier named Guardian. Daffodil, our fluffy amber cat, jumped on top of the fridge to get out of the way, and Prune Whip, our black-and-white cat, skittered across the floor and into the living room.

The kids turned on lights all over downstairs, and John called, "Can I turn on the Christmas tree lights?"

"Sure," I answered, "but light the fire first!"

I turned again to Evie, who simply stood in the middle of the big kitchen-dining room, not moving. "Evie, welcome. I'm sorry it's such chaos—let me take your coat." At first she resisted and then let me slip the worn material off her shoulders. Under the coat she wore a sweater and a plaid skirt; the skirt did not button, but was fastened with a pin, and for an obvious reason: Evie was not about to produce another Christmas baby, but she was very definitely pregnant.

Her eyes followed mine. Rather defiantly, she said, "That's why I'm here."

I thought of Evie's indifferent parents, and I thought about Christmas Eve. I put my arm around her for a gentle hug. "Tell me about it."

"Do I have to?"

"I think it might help, Evie."

Suzy, eight years old and still young enough to pull at my skirt and be whiny when she is tired, now did just that to get my full attention. "Let's put out the cookies and cocoa for Santa Claus *now.*"

Suddenly there was an anguished shout from the living room. "Come quick!" John yelled, and I went running.

Guardian was sitting under the tree, a long piece of green ribbon hanging from his mouth. Around him was a pile of Christmas wrappings, all nicely chewed. While we were in church, our visiting dog had unwrapped almost every single package under the tree.

Vicky said, "But we won't know who anything came from . . ."

Suzy burst into tears. "That dog has ruined it all!"

Evie followed us in. She was carrying Rob, who was sleeping with his head down on her shoulder. Father looked at her with his special warm glance that took in and assessed any situation. "Sit down, Evie," he ordered.

I took Rob from her, and when she had more or less collapsed in Wally's special chair, in front of the big fireplace, he asked, "When did you eat last?"

"I don't know. Yesterday, I think."

I dumped my sleeping child on the sofa and then headed for the kitchen, calling, "Vicky, Suzy, come help me make sandwiches. I'll warm up some soup. John, make up the couch in Daddy's office for Evie, please."

Our house is a typical square New England farmhouse. Upstairs are four bedrooms. Downstairs we have a big, rambling kitchen-dining room, all unexpected angles and nooks; a large, L-shaped living room and my husband's office, which he uses two nights a week for his patients in the nearby village. As I took a big jar of vegetable soup from the refrigerator and poured a good helping into a saucepan, I could hear my father's and Evie's voices, low, quiet, and I wondered if Evie was pouring out her story to him. I remembered hearing that her father seldom came home without stopping first at the tavern and that her mother had the reputation of being no better than she should be. And yet I knew that their response to Evie's pregnancy would be one of righteous moral indignation. To my daughters I said, "There's some egg salad in the fridge. Make a big sandwich for Evie."

I lifted the curtains and looked out the window. The roads would soon be impassable. I wanted my husband to be with us, in the warmth and comfort of our home.

I went back to the stove and poured a bowl of soup for Evie. Vicky and Suzy had produced a messy but edible sandwich and then gone off. I called Evie, and she sat at the table and began to eat hungrily. I sat beside her. "How did it happen? Do I know him?"

She shook her head. "No. His name's Billy. After we left here, I didn't feel—I didn't feel that anybody in the world loved me. I think that Mom and Pop are always happiest when I'm out of the house. When I was baby-sitting for you, I thought I saw what love was like. Mrs. Austin, I was lonely, I was so lonely it hurt. Then I met Billy, and I thought he loved me. So when he wanted to—I—but then I found out that it didn't have anything to do with love, at least not for Billy. When I got pregnant, he said, well, how did I even know it was his? Mrs. Austin, I never . . . never with anyone else. When he said that, I knew it was his way of telling me to get out, just like Mom and Pop."

The girls had wandered back into the kitchen while we were talking, and Suzy jogged at my elbow. "Why does Evie's tummy look so big?"

The phone rang. I called, "John, get it, please."

In a moment he came into the kitchen, looking slightly baffled. "It was someone from the hospital saying Dad's on his way home, and would we please make up the bed in the waiting room."

Evie looked up from her soup. "Mrs. Austin—" She turned her frightened face toward me, fearful, no doubt, that we were going to put her out.

"It's all right, Evie." I was thinking quickly. "John, would you mind sleeping in the guest room with Grandfather?"

"If Grandfather doesn't mind."

My father called from the living room, "Grandfather would enjoy John's company."

"All right then, Evie." I poured more soup into her bowl. "You can sleep in John's bed. Rob will love sharing his room with you."

"But who is Daddy bringing home?" John asked.

"What's wrong with Evie's tummy?" Suzy persisted.

"And why didn't Daddy tell us?" Vicky asked.

"Tell us what?" Suzy demanded.

"Who he's bringing home with him!" John said.

Evie continued to spoon soup into her mouth, at the same time struggling not to cry. I put one hand on her shoulder, and she reached up for it, asking softly, as the girls and John went into the living room, "Mrs. Austin, I knew you wouldn't turn me out on Christmas Eve, but what about . . . well, may I stay with you for a little while? I have some thinking to do."

"Of course you can, and you do have a lot of thinking to do—the future of your baby, for instance."

"I know. Now that it's getting so close, I'm beginning to get really scared. At first I thought I wanted the baby; I thought it would make Billy and me closer, make us a family like you and Dr. Austin and your kids, but now I know that was just wishful thinking. Sometimes I wish I could just go back, be your baby-sitter again. . . . Mrs. Austin, I just don't know what I'm going to do with a baby of my own."

I pressed her hand. "Evie, I know how you feel, but things have a way of working out. Try to stop worrying, at least tonight—it's Christmas Eve."

"And I'm home," Evie said. "I feel more at home in this house than anywhere else."

I thought of my own children and hoped that they would never have excuse to say that about someone else's house. To Evie I said, "Relax then, and enjoy Christmas. The decisions don't have to be made tonight."

My father ambled into the kitchen, followed by the three dogs. "I think the dogs are telling me they need to go out," he said. "I'll just walk around the house with them and see what the night is doing." He opened the kitchen door and let the dogs precede him.

I opened the curtains, not only to watch the progress of my father and the dogs, but to give myself a chance to think about Evie and how we could help her. More was needed, I knew, than just a few days' shelter. She had no money, no home, and a baby was on the way. . . . No wonder she looked scared—and trapped. I watched the falling snow and longed to hear the sound of my husband's car. Like Vicky, I wondered who on earth he was bringing home with him. Then I saw headlights coming up the road and heard a car slowing down, but the sound was not the slightly bronchial purr of Wally's car. Before I had a chance to wonder who it could be, the phone rang. "I'll get it!" Suzy yelled, and ran, beating Vicky. "Mother, it's Mrs. Underhill."

I went to the phone. Eugenia's voice came happily over the line. "Wasn't the Christmas Eve service beautiful! And did you see my teeth?" She laughed.

"You sang superbly, anyhow."

"Listen, why I called—you have two ovens, don't you?"

"Yes."

"Something's happened to mine. The burners work, but the oven is dead, and there's no way I can get anyone to fix it now. So what I wondered is, can I cook my turkey in one of your ovens?"

"Sure," I said, though I'd expected to use the second oven for the creamed-onion casserole and sweet potatoes—but how could I say no to Eugenia?

"Can I come over with my turkey now?" she asked. "I like to put it in a slow oven Christmas Eve, the way you taught me. Then I won't have to bother you again till tomorrow."

"Sure, Eugenia, come on over, but drive carefully."

"I will. Thanks," she said.

John murmured, "Just a typical Christmas Eve at the Austins," as the kitchen door opened, and my father and the dogs came bursting in, followed by a uniformed state trooper.

When Evie saw him, she looked scared.

My father introduced the trooper, who turned to me. "Mrs. Austin, I've been talking with your father here, and I think we've more or less sorted things out." Then he looked at Evie. "Young lady, we've been looking for you. We want to talk to you about your friends."

The color drained from her face.

"Don't be afraid," the trooper reassured her. "We just want to know where we can find you. I understand that you'll be staying with the Austins for a while—for the next few weeks, at least." He looked at my father, who nodded, and I wondered what the two had said to each other. Was Evie in more trouble than I thought?

She murmured something inaudible, keeping her eyes fastened to her soup.

"Well now, it's Christmas Eve," the trooper said, "and I'd like to be getting on home. It's bedtime for us all."

"We're waiting for Daddy," Suzy said. "He's on his way home."

"And he's bringing someone with him," Vicky added.

"Looks like you've got a full house," the trooper said. "Well, 'night, folks."

My father showed him out, then shut the door behind him.

"What was that—" John started to ask.

I quickly said, "What I want all of you to do is to go upstairs, right now, and get ready for bed. That's an order."

"But what about Daddy—"

"And whoever he's bringing—"

"And reading 'The Night Before Christmas' and Saint Luke—"

"And you haven't sung to us—"

I spoke through the clamor. "Upstairs. Now. You can come back down as soon as you're all ready for bed."

Evie rose. "Shall I get Rob?" I had the feeling she wanted to get away, escape my questions.

"We might as well leave him. Vicky, get Evie some nightclothes from my closet, please."

When they had all finally trooped upstairs, including Evie, I turned to my father who was perched on a stool by the kitchen counter. "All right, Dad, tell me about it," I said. "What did the officer tell you?"

"That soup smells mighty good," he said. I filled a bowl for him and waited.

Finally he said, "Evie was going with a bunch of kids who weren't much good. A couple of them were on drugs—not Evie, fortunately, or her boyfriend. And they stole some cars, just for kicks, and then abandoned them. The police are pretty sure that Evie wasn't in-volved, but they want to talk to her and her friends, and they've been trying to round them up. They went to her parents' house looking for her. Her mother and father made it seem as if she'd run away—they didn't mention that they'd put her out. All they did was denounce her, but they did suggest she might have come here."

"Poor Evie. There's so much good in her, and sometimes I wonder how, with her background. What did you tell the trooper?"

"I told him Evie was going to stay with you and Wally for the time being, that you would take responsibility for her. They still want to talk to her, but I convinced him to wait until after Christmas. I guess the trooper figured that, as long as she's with you, she would be looked after and out of harm's way."

"Thank goodness. All she needs is to be hauled into a station house on Christmas Eve—" Just then the heavy knocker on the kitchen door banged.

It was Eugenia, with a large turkey in a roasting pan in her arms. "I'll just pop it in the oven," she said. "If you think about basting it when you baste yours, okay, but it'll do all right by itself. Hey you don't have yours in yet!"

What with one thing and another, I'd forgotten our turkey, but it was prepared and ready in the cold pantry. I whipped out and brought it in and put it in the other oven.

As Eugenia drove off, the dogs started with their welcoming bark, and I heard the sound of Wally's engine.

The children heard, too, and came rushing downstairs. "Wait!" I ordered. "Don't mob Daddy. And remember he has someone with him."

Evie came slowly downstairs, wrapped in an old blue plaid robe of mine. John opened the kitchen door, and the dogs went galloping out.

"Whoa! Down!" I could hear my husband command. And then, to the children, "Make way!" The children scattered, and Wally came in, his arm around a young woman whom I had never seen before. She was holding a baby in her arms.

"This is Maria Heraldo," Wally said. "Maria, my wife, Victoria. And—" He looked at the infant.

"Pepita," she said, "After her father."

Wally took the babe. "Take off your coat," he said to the mother. "Maria's husband was killed in an accident at work two weeks ago. Her family is all in South America, and she was due to be released from the hospital today. Christmas Eve didn't seem to me to be a very good time for her to be alone."

I looked at the baby, who had an amazing head of dark hair. "She isn't the baby—"

"That I delivered tonight? No, though that little boy was slow in coming—that's why we're so late." He smiled down at the young woman. "Pepita was born a week ago." He looked up and saw our children hovering in the doorway, Evie and my father behind them. When he saw Evie, he raised his eyebrows in a questioning gesture.

"Evie's going to be staying with us for a while," I told him. Explanations would come later. "Maria, would you like some soup?"

"I would," my husband said, "and Maria will have some too." He glanced at the children. "Vicky and Suzy, will you go up to the attic, please, and bring down the cradle?"

They were off like a flash.

My husband questioned the young mother. "Tired?"

"No. I slept while the little boy was being delivered. So did Pepita." And she looked with radiant pride at her daughter who was sleeping again.

"Then let's all go into the living room and warm ourselves in front of the fire. We have some Christmas traditions you might like to share with us."

The young woman gazed up at him, at me, "I'm so grateful to you—"

"Nonsense. Come along."

Then Maria saw Evie, and I watched her eyes flick to Evie's belly, then upward, and the two young women exchanged a long look. Evie's glance shifted to the sleeping child, and then she held out her arms. Maria gently handed her the baby, and Evie took the child and cradled it in her arms. For the first time that evening, a look of peace seemed to settle over her features.

It is not easy for a woman to raise a child alone, and Maria would probably go back to her family. In any case, her child had obviously been conceived in love, and even death could not take that away. Evie's eyes were full of tears as she carried Pepita into the living room, but she no longer looked so lost and afraid, and I had the feeling that whatever happened, Evie would be able to handle it. She would have our help—Wally's and mine—for as long as she needed it, but something told me that she wouldn't need it for long.

In a short while, Maria was ensconced in one of the big chairs, a bowl of soup on the table beside her. Evie put the baby in the cradle, and knelt, rocking it gently. Wally sat on the small sofa with Rob in his lap, a mug of soup in one hand. The two girls were curled up on the big davenport, one on either side of their grandfather, who had his arms around them. I sat across from Maria, and Evie came and sat on the footstool by me. John was on the floor in front of the fire. The only light was from the Christmas tree and the flickering flames of the fire. On the mantel were a cup of cocoa and a plate of cookies.

"Now," my husband said, "'Twas the night before Christmas, when all through the house . . .'"

When he had finished, with much applause from the children and Evie and Maria, he looked to me. "Your turn."

John jumped up and handed me my guitar. I played and sang "I Wonder as I Wander," and then "In the Bleak Midwinter," and ended up with "Let All Mortal Flesh Keep Silence." As I put the guitar away, I saw Maria reach out for Evie, and the two of them briefly clasped hands.

"And now," Wally said, "your turn, please, Grandfather."

My father opened his Bible and began to read. When he came to "And she brought forth her firstborn son, and wrapped him in swaddling clothes, and laid him in a manger; because there was no room for them in the inn," I looked at Maria, who was rocking the cradle with her foot while her baby murmured in her sleep. Evie, barely turning, keeping her eyes fastened on the sleeping infant, leaned her head against my knee, rubbing her cheek against the wool of my skirt.

Suzy was sleeping with her head down in her grandfather's lap, while he continued to read: "And suddenly there was with the angel a multitude of the heavenly host praising God, and saying, Glory to God in the highest, and on earth peace, good will toward men."

I remembered John saying, "Just a typical Christmas Eve at the Austins," and I wondered if there ever could be such a thing as a typical Christmas. For me, each one is unique. This year our house was blessed by Evie and her unborn child, by Eugenia's feeling free to come and put her turkey in our stove, and by Maria and Pepita's turning our plain New England farmhouse into a stable.

Christmas Gifts

And what, Lord, do you have for me?
Only a baby, helpless and small.
Shall I sit beneath this tree
And rock him till he grows up tall?

Only a baby, only a boy,
Not a mighty king or queen.
I will rock him in my joy
Underneath the tree's full green.

And what, Lord, do I have for you?
Only my arms to hold the child
Safe from winds now hurling through
The branches in this winter wild.

Only my heart, only my arms
Open to receive All Love.
How can I keep the child from harm?
How shall I all ills remove?

Child who is Love, beneath the tree
I'll sit and rock the whole night through.
Oh, what, Lord, do you have for me?
Only yourself, Lord. Only *you*.

Tree at Christmas

The children say the tree must reach the ceiling,
And so it does, angel on topmost branch,
Candy canes and golden globes and silver chains,
Trumpets that toot, and birds with feathered tails.
Each year we say, each year we fully mean:
"This is the loveliest tree of all." This tree
Bedecked with love and tinsel reaches heaven.
A pagan throwback may have brought it here
Into our room, and yet these decked-out boughs
Can represent those other trees, the one
Through which we fell in pride, when Eve forgot
That freedom is man's freedom to obey
And to adore, not to replace the light
With disobedient darkness and self-will.
On Twelfth Night when we strip the tree
And see its branches bare and winter cold
Outside the comfortable room, the tree
Is then the tree on which all darkness hanged,
Completing the betrayal that began
With that first stolen fruit. And then, O God,
This is the tree that Simon bore uphill,
This is the tree that held all love and life.
Forgive us, Lord, forgive us for that tree.
But now, still decked, bedecked, in joy arrayed
For these great days of Christmas thanks and song.
This is the tree that lights our faltering way,
For when man's first and proud rebellious act
Had reached its nadir on that hill of skulls
These shining, glimmering boughs remind us that
The knowledge that we stole was freely given
And we were sent the spirit's radiant strength
That we might know all things. We grasp for truth
And lose it till it comes to us by love.
The glory of Lebanon shines on this Christmas tree,
The tree of life that opens wide the gates.
The children say the tree must reach the ceiling,
And so it does: for me the tree has grown so high
It pierces through the vast and star-filled sky.

Royal Alchemy

piphany. "No longer do the magi bring presents to the moon and the stars, for this child made the moon and the stars."

These words were copied into my Goody Book (a big old "commonplace book" in which, for many years, I have copied out words that have stimulated and challenged me); I wrote down these words a long time ago, and where they came from or who wrote them I don't remember. Who were the magi? the magicians, the three wise men who came from far away to bring gifts to the child Jesus?

My bishop suggested that they were alchemists, and that when they brought their gifts they were giving Jesus their magic. Gold, frankincense, and myrrh are all part of the alchemical ingredients. At the time of this conversation, one of my granddaughters lent me a novel which had a lot in it about alchemy; what intrigued me especially was the suggestion that alchemists cared far more about reconciling male and female than they did about changing metal into gold.

Reconciling male and female: first, within ourselves, then, with each other. Perhaps this reconciliation was the priceless gift the magi gave to Jesus, along with the gold, frankincense, and myrrh, and it was a much greater gift than the three tangible ones. Jesus accepted the gifts, and in turn gave the greatest of the gifts to us. In a world where women were far less than second-class citizens, he chose women for his closest friends—Mary of Magdala, Mary and Martha of Bethany. He spoke to a Samaritan woman at a well, breaking three taboos: Men did not speak publicly to women, most certainly not to a Samaritan woman, and no good Jew would at that time have taken water from a Samaritan. Samaritans worshipped God differently from the Jews; they even worshipped on the wrong mountain. They were far more suspect than people from a different denomination. They did not belong. The woman at the well was awed by the gifts Jesus gave her, even the gift of loving acceptance. In her brokenness, she was able to receive the reconciliation of Jesus' healing.

In his living, his speaking, his action, Jesus offered the world the reconciliation the wise men had brought to him as their greatest gift and, alas, the world could not accept it then, and still, today, cannot. We are still part of that brokenness that split us asunder eons ago in the garden.

Is it not likely that if Adam and Eve had known how to wait, had trusted God's timing, that at the right moment God would have come to them? God would have come to them saying, "Here children, here is the fruit of the tree of knowledge of good and evil. You're ready for it. Eat."

But the serpent tempted them to be impatient, to break time, to rush into graduate school physics courses and depth psychology before they'd learned how to read.

Perhaps at the right moment God would have called Adam and Eve, saying, "The time has come for you to leave the safety of this beautiful garden where you have learned all that you can learn in this place. It is time for you to go out into the rest of the world." It would have been somewhat like the mother bird urging the fledglings out of the nest when they're ready to fly. But Adam and Eve weren't yet ready to fly, and we've been lumbering about on the ground ever since.

Of course that is a story, but it's a story that works for me, and one reason stories are icons for us human beings is that they are our best way of struggling to comprehend the incomprehensible. We do not know why our psyches are out of sync, but the story of Adam and Eve gives us creative glimpses.

When Descartes said, "I think, therefore I am," he did us no favor, but further fragmented us, making us limit ourselves to the cognitive at the expense of the imaginative and the intuitive. But each time we read the Gospels we are offered anew this healing reconciliation, and, if we will, we can accept the most wondrous gift of the magi.

My icon is the glory of the heavens at night, a cold, clear night when the stars are more brilliant than diamonds. The wise men looked at the stars, and what they saw called them away from their comfortable dwellings and towards Bethlehem. When I look at the stars, I see God's glory in the wonder of creation.

The stars can become idols when we look to them for counsel, which should come only from God. For the magi, astronomy and astrology were one science, and it is probably a very sad thing that they ever became separated.

That is yet another schism which looks for healing, and we have not been as wise as the three magi who came from their far corners of the world, seeking the new King, the king who was merely a child.

Surely if the world is as interdependent as the discoveries of particle physics imply, then what happens among the stars does make a difference to our daily lives. But the stars will not and should not tell us the future. They are not to be worshipped. Like the wise men, we no longer bring presents to the moon and the stars, for this Child made the moon and the stars. Alleluia!

Joy

We are moving soberly towards the new year, joy for an anguished world.

For Dana

The end of the year is here. We are at a new beginning.
A birth has come, and we reenact
At its remembrance the extraordinary fact
Of our unique, incomprehensible being.

The new year has started, for moving and growing.
The child's laugh within and through the adult's tears,
In joy and incomprehension at the singing years
Pushes us into fresh life, new knowing.

Here at the end of the year comes the year's springing.
The falling and melting snow meet in the stream
That flows with living waters and cleanses the dream.
The reed bends and endures and sees the dove's winging.

Move into the year and the new time's turning
Open and vulnerable and loving and steady.
The stars are aflame; creation is ready.
The day is at hand: the bright sun burns.

Saying Yes

One New Year's Eve I was allowed, for the first time, to stay up with my parents until midnight. I remember only one thing about that milestone: While the village clock was striking twelve, Father opened his small new engagement diary for the year, and we all signed our names in it. It was Father's way of saying *yes* to Mother and to me and to the new year, no matter what it might bring. It would have been much easier for him to withdraw from it, as he occasionally withdrew from the pain with whiskey, but he refused to withdraw, and I knew this without understanding it in the least, and was grateful as I added my signature to Mother's and his.

Joyful in the newness of the heart

7 January 1979

Joyful in the newness of the heart,
Astonished by love's blazing light,
Making an end to a new start,
Early to smile, swift & bright.
Singing His love, all night, all night.

Peace in the midst of chaos comes
Alert & lively, he's on the ready.
Remarkable, hearing different drums,
keeps open, & waiting, & steady.
Surely, surely the depths he plumbs

May the new year bring love, bring peace,
On the Close, the Cathedral, The loving heart
Ready for angels, looking for light,
Thinking of others, That pain may cease,
Often in prayer, by day, by night
Nurtured in love: may his joy increase!

A Winter's Walk

There is enough ground cover of snow to provide traction, and I have on good hiking boots. The dogs rush ahead, double back, rush ahead again. Once we are into the woods, the wind drops and it is less cold. We get to the stone bridge over the brook, which is still running under its icy edges despite the subfreezing weather. To the right of the brook is the first and smaller of two remarkable beaver dams. We follow around the rim of the frozen pond to the larger dam, an amazing feat of engineering. The pond gleams silver. The winter light slants through the trees. We don't talk much, except to remark on some particular beauty or other—the light on the icicles near the first dam, a small bird's nest in a low cleft of a tree.

Then we tramp home to make cocoa and warm our toes. And think a little about the past year. There has been considerable personal grief. It has not been a good year for many of our friends. For the planet it has been an astounding year. The world events that shared the news with Hurricane Bob when I was first home from the hospital in San Diego have continued to accelerate. There is no more Soviet Union. The communist religion has gone down the drain with unprecedented rapidity. The bitter fighting between Serbs and Croats continues, the differences in religion making the fight more anguished.

What will happen in the next year is far from clear.

The Gift of Christ

Instead of being allowed to grieve for the precariousness of all life, we are often taught to look for a security that does not exist. No one can promise that we will end a day in safety, that we, or someone dear to us, will not be hurt.

All too often we fall for it and go into debt to buy the latest gadget. Whatever it is, it's made to self-destruct after a few years, and it will never help whatever it is that's making us hurt.

What does help? The gift of Christ, who offers us the grieving that is healing. This kind of grieving is a gift; it helps us "Walk that lonesome valley." It involves a lifelong willingness to accept the gift, which is part of what Bonhoeffer called *costly grace.*

We were bought with a price, and what has cost God so much cannot be cheap for us.

The search for grace, costly grace, involves the acceptance of pain and the creative grief which accompanies growth into maturity. Don't be afraid the pain will destroy the wholeness. It leads, instead, to the kind of wholeness that rejoices in Resurrection.

We live in a time where costly grace is what makes life bearable; more than bearable—joyful and creative, so that even our grief is part of our partnership in co-creation with God.

The world around us is full of racial tension; the problems of starvation across the globe grow greater with each year; the planet is still torn apart by war; the result of our technocratic affluence is an earth depleted, an air polluted, and a population suffering from more mental illness, suicide, and despair than our country has ever known. So perhaps we finally have to accept that the great do-it-yourself dream hasn't worked, and we've been dreaming wrong, dreaming nightmares. The original dream had to do with a wholeness which touched every part of our lives, including grief, and it had to do with grace, costly grace.

Moving Towards Lent

It is still winter. Today has seen a quick flurry of snow followed by blue skies and sunshine. We are moving towards Lent and then the glory of Easter, that most marvelous holy day that radiantly bursts through the limitations of fact.

All Heaven with its power*

Lord Jesus, in this fateful hour
I place all Heaven with its power
And the sun with its brightness
And the snow with its whiteness
And the fire with all the strength it hath
And the lightning with its rapid wrath
And the winds with their swiftness along their path
And the sea with its deepness
And the rocks with their steepness
And the child in the manger
Sharing our danger
And the man sandal-shod
Revealing our God
And the hill with its cross
To cry grief, pain, and loss
And the dark empty tomb
Like a Heavenly womb
Giving birth to true life
While death howls in strife
And the bread and the wine
Making human divine
And the stars with their singing
And cherubim winging
And Creation's wild glory
Contained in His story
And the hope of new birth
On this worn stricken earth
And His coming, joy-streaming
Creation redeeming
And the earth with its starkness
All these we place
By God's Almighty Help and grace
Between ourselves and the powers of darkness.

*This poem is based on and incorporates "The Rune of St. Patrick."

Prayers for Peace

We send you all our prayers for peace in our hearts and in the world, for an end to terrorism and famine, and for the birth of hope and loving connections among all people.

Celebration

Let us, seeing, celebrate

The glory of Love's incarnate birth

And sing its joy to all the world.

—from "Love's incarnate birth"

Love's incarnate birth

Observe and contemplate.
Make real. Bring to be.
Because we note the falling tree
The sound is truly heard.
Look! The sunrise! Wait—
It needs us to look, to see,
To hear, and speak the Word.

Observe and contemplate
The cosmos and our little earth.
Observing, we affirm the worth
Of sun and stars and light unfurled.
So, let us, seeing, celebrate
The glory of Love's incarnate birth
And sing its joy to all the world.

Observe and contemplate.
Make real. Affirm. Say Yes,
And in this season sing and bless
Wind, ice, snow; rabbit and bird;
Comet, and quark; things small and great.
Oh, observe and joyfully confess
The birth of Love's most lovely Word.

Most amazing Word

Thank you, God, for being born,
You who first invented birth
(Universe, galaxies, the earth).
When your world was tired & worn
You came laughing on the morn.

Thank you, most amazing Word
For your silence in the womb
Where there was so little room
Yet the still small voice was heard
Throughout a planet dark & blurred.

Merry Christmas! Wondrous day!
Maker of the universe,
You the end, & you the source
Come to share in human clay
And, yourself, to show the Way.

First coming

He did not wait till the world was ready,
till men and nations were at peace.
He came when the Heavens were unsteady,
and prisoners cried out for release.

He did not wait for the perfect time.
He came when the need was deep and great.
He dined with sinners in all their grime,
turned water into wine. He did not wait

till hearts were pure. In joy he came
to a tarnished world of sin and doubt.
To a world like ours, of anguished shame
he came, and his Light would not go out.

He came to a world which did not mesh,
to heal its tangles, shield its scorn.
In the mystery of the Word made Flesh
the Maker of the stars was born.

We cannot wait till the world is sane
to raise our songs with joyful voice,
for to share our grief, to touch our pain,
He came with Love: Rejoice! Rejoice!

Gratitude

New Year's Eve was very quiet, just Bion and Laurie and me. Laurie was on call, so we went to bed early and I turned out my light about midnight. I made no resolutions, which, like Lenten resolves, are best looked at lightly. I thanked God that we've had the strength to get through this year, which has been very hard on almost all the people I love best. I prayed for the world. The best way to help the world is to start by loving each other, not blandly, blindly, but realistically, with understanding and forbearance and forgiveness. I'm very proud of those closest to me, for their dignity, courage, forbearance. I am grateful indeed for my friends, who go on bravely keeping the stars in their courses. I pray for those who have joined the mighty cloud of witnesses.

Such Smallness

Particle physics has a sense of the absolute significance of the very small, the so incredibly small we can't even imagine such smallness.

In *Particles,* Michael Chester writes, "Not only does [the neutrino] have zero charge, it has zero mass. The neutrino is a spinning little bit of nothingness that travels at the speed of light."

I love that! A spinning little bit of nothingness! It so delights me that I wrote a Christmas song about it.

> The neutrino and the unicorn
> Danced the night that Christ was born.
> A spinning little bit of nothingness
> that travels at the speed of light
> an unseen spark of somethingness
> is all that can hold back the night.
> The tiny neutron split in two,
> an electron and a proton form.
> Where is the energy that is lost?
> Who can hold back the impending storm?
> Cosmic collapse would be the cost.
> A spinning nothing, pure and new,
> The neutrino comes to heal and bless.
> The neutrino and the unicorn
> danced the night that Christ was born.
> The sun is dim, the stars are few,
> The earthquake comes to split and shake.
> All purity of heart is lost,
> In the black density of night
> stars fall. O will the heavens break?
> Then through the tingling of black frost
> the unicorn in silver dress
> crosses the desert, horn alight.
> Earth's plates relax their grinding stress.
> The unicorn comes dancing to
> make pure again, redeem and bless,
> The neutrino and the unicorn
> danced the night that Christ was born.

A Call to Jury Duty

n the late afternoon, when the long December night had already darkened the skies, we opened Christmas cards, taking turns, reading the messages, enjoying this once-a-year being in touch with far-flung friends. There, incongruously lying among the Christmas greetings, was an official-looking envelope addressed to me, with *Clerk of Court, New York County,* in the upper left-hand corner. A call to jury duty. Manhattan does not give its prospective jurors much notice. My call was for the first week in January. To the notice inside had been added the words *Must Serve*.

It wasn't the first time that my call had read *Must Serve*. A few months earlier I had written from Minnesota to the Clerk of Court, New York County, explaining that I was not trying to avoid jury duty, that I had previously served on a panel under a fine woman judge, and that I was ready and willing to serve again. But I pointed out, as I had already done several times before, that I do a good bit of lecturing which takes me far from New York, and I gave the Clerk of Court several dates when I would be available, sighing internally because bureaucracy never called me on the weeks that I offered.

This time they did.

So I relaxed and enjoyed Christmas in the country, at Crosswicks, bitter cold outside, warmth of firelight and candlelight within, and laughter and conversation and the delectable smells of roasting and baking. One of the highlights came on Christmas Day itself, with the mercury falling far below zero, when my husband went out into the winter garden and picked brussels sprouts, commenting as he brought them in triumphantly, "Mr. Birdseye never froze them like this," and we had brussels sprouts out of our own garden with Christmas dinner.

And then, before Twelfth Night, I was back in New York again, taking the subway downtown to the criminal court to which I had been assigned. I took plenty of work with me, because I had been told that lawyers do not like writers. But just as had happened on my previous jury duty, I got chosen as a juror on the second day.

The case was an ugly one, involving assault in the second degree, which means possession of a dangerous weapon, with intent to cause injury or death.

Two men were sitting in the courtroom as defendants. They looked at the twelve of us who had been told to stay in our seats in the jury box—looked at us with cold eyes, with arrogance, even with contempt. Later, as we jurors got to know each other, we admitted that we were afraid of them. And yet, according to our judicial system, we had been put in the position of having to decide whether or not, according to the law, these men were guilty as charged.

I was fortunate to serve again under a highly intelligent woman judge, who warned us that we must set aside our emotions. What we felt about the defendants should not enter into our deliberations. We should not form any preconceived opinions. "And remember," she told us, "these two men and their lawyers do not have to prove to you that they are innocent. They do not have to appear on the witness stand. The burden of proof is on the assistant district attorney. The American way is that these two men are innocent, unless it can be proved, beyond a reasonable doubt, that they are guilty. This is the American way." She also pointed out that this assumption of innocence unless guilt can be proven is not the way of the rest of the world, of countries behind the Iron Curtain or in much of South America, where the assumption is that you are guilty unless, somehow or other, by persuasion or bribe, you can prove your innocence.

When I was called for jury duty, I knew that I would be taking two long subway rides each day, and riding the subway in Manhattan is nothing one does for pleasure. So I picked up a small book from one of my piles of Books To Be Read Immediately. Why did I pick this book at this particular time? I don't know. But I have found that often I will happen on a book just at the time when I most need to hear what it has to say.

This book couldn't have been more apt. It was *Revelation and Truth*, by Nicholas Berdyaev. I didn't do much reading the first day because I was sent from court to court, but once I was on a jury and had long periods of time in the jury room, I opened the book, surrounded by my fellow jurors who were reading, chatting, doing needlework or crossword puzzles. There couldn't have been a better place than a criminal court in which to read Berdyaev's words telling me that one of the gravest problems in the Western world today is that we have taken a forensic view of God.

Forensic: *to do with crime*. I first came across the word in an English murder mystery. Forensic medicine is medicine having to do with crime. The coroner needs to find out if the victim has been shot,

stabbed, or poisoned. Was the crime accidental, self-inflicted, murder? Criminal medicine.

And there I was, in a criminal court, being warned by a Russian theologian that God is not like a judge sentencing a criminal. Yet far too often we view God as an angry judge who assumes that we are guilty unless we can placate divine ire and establish our innocence. This concept seemed especially ironic after the judge's warning that this is not the American way of justice.

How did the Western world fall into such a gloomy and unscriptural misapprehension?

I suspect there may have been a lingering shadow of God as a cold and unforgiving judge—not a judge who believes in the American way, but one who assumes our guilt.

But no, Berdyaev states emphatically, no, that is not God, not the God of Scripture who over and over again shows love for us imperfect creatures, who does not demand that we be good or virtuous before we can be loved. When we stray from God, it is not God's pleasure to punish us. It is God's pleasure to welcome us back, and then throw a party in celebration of our homecoming.

God says through the prophet Hosea,

> *All my compassion is aroused,*
> *I will not carry out my fierce anger,*
> *I will not destroy Ephraim again,*
> *for I am God, not man:*
> *I am the Holy One in your midst,*
> *and have no wish to destroy.*

The nature of God does not fluctuate. The One who made us is still the Creator, the Rejoicer, the Celebrator, who looks at what has been made, and calls it good.

After the guard summoned us from the jury room to the court room, I sat in the jury box and looked at those two men who were there because they were destroyers rather than creators. They had used sharp knives, destructively; their intention had been to injure, or kill. I wasn't at all sure I wanted to be at the same celebration with them. They both had long hair, one head dark and greasy, the other brown and lank. They looked as though they had strayed out of the sixties, hippies who had grown chronologically, but not in any other way. It was difficult to abide by the judge's warning and not form any opinion of them until all the evidence was in.

That evening I was tired, mentally as well as physically. I bathed, then sat in my quiet corner to read Evening Prayer. For the Old

Testament lesson I was reading the extraordinary story of Jacob's ladder of angels ascending and descending, linking earth and heaven, the Creation and the Creator, in glorious interdependence.

God stood above the ladder of angels, and said:

> *I am the Lord God of Abraham, your father, and the God of Isaac: the land that you are lying on, to you will I give it, and to your seed. And your seed shall be as the dust of the earth. . . . And behold, I am with you, and will keep you in all the places where you go, and will bring you again to this land, for I will not leave you, until I have done that which I have said.*
>
> *And Jacob woke out of his sleep, and he said, Surely the Lord is in this place, and I knew it not.*
>
> *And he was afraid, and said, How dreadful is this place! This is none other than the house of God, and this is the gate of heaven.*

For Jacob the house of God was not a building, not an enclosure, but an open place with earth for the floor; heaven for the roof.

So Jacob took the desert stone he had used for a pillow and upon which he had dreamed the angelic dream, and set it up for a pillar, and poured oil upon the top of it. Oil—precious, sacramental.

How glorious stars must have been all those centuries ago when the planet was not circled by a corona of light from all our cities, by smog from our internal combustion engines. Jacob, lying on the ground, the stone under his head, would have seen the stars as we cannot see them today. Perhaps we have thrown up a smoke screen between ourselves and the angels.

But Jacob would not have been blinded to the glory of the stars as part of the interdependence of the desert, the human being, the smallest insects, all part of Creation.

If we look at the makeup of the word disaster, dis-aster, we see *dis*, which means separation, and *aster*, which means star. So dis-aster is separation from the stars. Such separation is disaster indeed. When we are separated from the stars, the sea, each other, we are in danger of being separated from God.

That January evening after the first tiring day as a juror, after I had read the story of Jacob and the angels, I turned to the New Testament, to read from the ninth chapter of Matthew's Gospel, where Jesus had called Matthew from collecting taxes. In Israel in those days, a tax collector worked for the hated Romans, rather than for an equivalent of the I.R.S. We don't have any analogy for the kind of tax collector Matthew was. But because they were employed by the enemy, all tax collectors were scum.

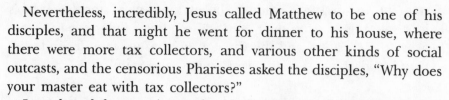

Nevertheless, incredibly, Jesus called Matthew to be one of his disciples, and that night he went for dinner to his house, where there were more tax collectors, and various other kinds of social outcasts, and the censorious Pharisees asked the disciples, "Why does your master eat with tax collectors?"

Jesus heard the question and said, "It is not the healthy who need a doctor, but the sick. Go and learn the meaning of the words, *What I want is mercy, not sacrifice.*" He was quoting from the prophet Hosea. And he went on, "And indeed I have not come to call the virtuous, but sinners."

I'm uneasy about self-conscious virtue. It implies that the virtuous person is in control, keeps all the laws, has all the answers, always knows what is right and what is wrong. It implies a conviction which enables the virtuous person to feel saved, while the rest of the world is convicted.

Probably it was because I was on jury duty that I noticed the paradoxical connections between the words conviction, convince, convicted, *con*vict (noun), and con*vict* (verb). If we assume that we are virtuous, particularly when we set our virtue against someone else's sin, we are proclaiming a forensic, crime-and-punishment theology, not a theology of love. The Pharisees who did not like to see Jesus eating with sinners wanted virtue—virtue which consisted in absolute obedience to the law.

The Pharisees were not bad people, remember. They were good. They were virtuous. They did everything the Moral Majority considers moral. They knew right from wrong, and they did what was right. They went regularly to the services in the temple. They tithed, and they didn't take some off the top for income tax or community services or increased cost-of-living expenses. They were, in fact, what many Christians are calling the rest of us to be: good, moral, virtuous, and sure of being saved.

So what was wrong? Dis-aster. Separation from the stars, from the tax collectors, the Samaritans, from the publican who beat his breast and knew himself to be a sinner. The Pharisees, not all of them, but some of them, looked down on anybody who was less moral, less virtuous than they were. They assumed that their virtue ought to be rewarded and the sin of others punished.

If we twelve jurors found those two men guilty as charged, they would be punished by the state. They would likely be put in prison: forensic punishment. Necessary in our judicial system, perhaps, but Berdyaev warned that we should not think of God's ways as being judicial. God is a God of love.

When I looked at those two cruel-faced men, I had to remind myself that they were God's children, and that they were loved. If they had committed the crime of which they were accused, it would cause God grief, not anger.

I sat in the jury room with the radiators hissing and the January cold pressing against the windows, hearing the constant sound of taxis and busses and cars honking on the streets below.

I'm not at all sure that the state's forensic punishment is punishment at all. It may be deterrence, or an attempt to protect the innocent. I have no desire to go all wishy-washy and bleeding-heart about the rapist who is let off with an easy sentence so that he can then go out and rape and kill again, as statistics prove is almost inevitable. Our jails may be deplorable, our courts overcrowded and years behind schedule; our lawyers are not knights in shining armour; but we do what we can, in our blundering way, to curb crime and violence, and our top-heavy system remains one of the best on the planet.

But our own need for law and our system of prosecution and sentencing does not produce true punishment, because true punishment should result in penitence. Real punishment produces an acceptance of wrongdoing, a repugnance for what has been done, confession, and an honest desire to amend. Real punishment comes to me when I weep tears of grief because I have let someone down. The punishment is not inflicted by anyone else. My own recognition and remorse for what I have done is the worst punishment I could possibly have.

Perhaps the most poignant moment for me in all of Scripture comes after Peter has denied Jesus three times, and Jesus turns and looks at him. That loving look must have been far worse punishment for Peter than any number of floggings. And he went out and wept bitterly.

Jacob, too, learned to weep bitterly, but he was an old man before he came to an understanding of himself which included acceptance of repentance without fear.

This is something a criminal court is not equipped to cope with. The judge and the lawyers and the jurors are there to learn the facts as accurately as possible, and to interpret them according to the law. Forensically.

It is impossible to interpret the story of Jacob in this way. Jacob does outrageous things, and instead of being punished, he is rewarded. He bargains with God shamelessly:

"*If* God will be with me, and will keep me in this way that I go, and will give me bread to eat, and raiment to put on, so that I come again to my father's house in peace; *then* shall the Lord be my God."

Jacob also agrees to tithe, but only if God does for him all that

he asks. He cheats, but he knows that he cheats; he never tries to fool himself into thinking that he is more honest than he is. He openly acknowledges his fear of Esau's revenge.

And yet, with all his shortcomings, he is a lovable character, and perhaps we recognize ourselves in him with all his complexity. He has an extraordinary sense of awe—an awe which does not demand fairness, an awe which is so profound a response to the Creator that it cannot be sustained for long periods of time.

But whenever El Shaddai came to Jacob, he was ready for the Presence. That was why he took his stone pillow and built an altar. Jacob knew delight in the Lord in a spontaneous manner which too many of us lose as we move out of childhood. And because we have forgotten delight, we are unable to accept the golden light of the angels.

Three centuries ago Thomas Traherne wrote:

> *Should God give himself and all worlds to you, and you refuse them, it would be to no purpose. Should He love you and magnify you, should He give His Son to die for you, and command all angels and men to love you, should He exalt you in His throne and give you dominion over all His works and you neglect them, it would be to no purpose.*
>
> *Should He make you in His image, and employ all His Wisdom and power to fill eternity with treasures, and you despise them, it would be in vain. In all these things you have to do; and therefore all your actions are great and magnificent, being of infinite importance in all eyes; while all creatures stand in expectation of what will be the result of your liberty. . . . It is by your love that you enjoy all His delights, and are delightful to Him.*

As I live with Jacob's story I see that there is far more to him than the smart cheat, the shallow manipulator. There are many times when he so enjoyed the delights of God, that he himself became delightful.

How often are we delightful to God? How marvelous that we are called delightful!

We are not meant to cringe before God. We are to enjoy all the delights which the Lord has given us, sunsets and sunrises, and a baby's first laugh, and friendship and love, and the brilliance of the stars. Enjoying the Creator's delights implies connectedness.

And so there is hope that we, too, may so enjoy all the delights that God has given us, that we may truly be delightful.

Eighty-Second Street

When I remember the years in the apartment on Eighty-second Street, it is mostly the good things that I remember at home, and the bad at school. When I look at the apartment in my mind's eye, it is likely to be Christmas. This was the time when Father lifted from the physical pain in which he constantly lived, and the equally acute pain of knowing that his postwar work was not as successful as his earlier work. I did not understand my father's pain, but I knew that at Christmastime the apartment, instead of being heavy and dark, became sparkling and light as champagne, with Father sneaking home with an armload of presents, and writing stocking poems, and believing (I think) for a few weeks in a future in which there was hope.

Homemade Decorations

Christmas was white this year—we had two feet of snow—with bitter cold winds, and the branches of the stripped trees like dark lace against a white sky—the first really Christmassy weather we've had for a long time. Crosswicks was filled with music, and the wonderful smell of the Christmas tree, full of ornaments that span decades, some going back to my childhood. There is one small strand of tiny, homemade silver balls, from my twelfth Christmas which was in Chamonix, Mont Blanc, where all our decorations were homemade.

Chamonix

That month in Chamonix was an ambiguous one for me. When I could, I reacted as a child, but I was being forced into growing up. I wanted to balance the pain of school with comfort, safety, changelessness, but I found pain, discovery, change. I listened to Mother playing Bach on a barely playable upright piano, and I watched her play solitaire. Because she could not understand Father, neither could I, and I was drawn into her unhappiness.

And yet that Christmas was one of our loveliest. All the decorations on the small tree were homemade. We still hang on our Christmas tree each year a small silver chain made of little beads of tinfoil, rolled from the paper in Father's packages of Sphinx cigarettes. We cut pictures out of the English illustrated magazines to replace the horrors on the wall which came with the rented villa. My presents were the very books I had asked for, plus colored pencils and a fresh box of watercolors and a new notebook with a marbleized cover. What we ate for Christmas dinner I don't remember; all we ate that winter, it seemed, was rabbit, which was plentiful and cheap; and Berthe, the eighteen-year-old girl Mother had brought with her from Publier (for, even that austere winter, she managed to have help), cooked rabbit every conceivable way. And a few inconceivable, Father would add. We also ate hearts of palm; for some reason the village grocer had an overabundance of this delicacy, and needed to unload it. Berthe bargained with him and came home triumphantly with string bags bulging with cans.

The Twenty-Four Days
Before Christmas: An Austin
Family Story

December is probably my favorite month.

And on the first day of December we were out of bed before Mother came to call us.

I ran to the window to see if maybe it had snowed during the night. But the ground was still bare, the grass tawny, with a few last leaves fluttering over it. The trees were shaking dark branches against a grey sky.

"Any snow?" Suzy asked. Suzy's my little sister. She's only four, and I've just turned seven. I can read. Of course, so can John. He's ten. I answered, "Not a smidgin. And the sky isn't white enough for snow today. But it doesn't matter—it's the first day December!"

One of the reasons we love December so is Christmas, not only that Christmas is coming, but that we do something special every single day of the month to prepare for the twenty-fifth day.

John was up and out of the house before Suzy and I were dressed. He has a paper route, every morning before breakfast, and he's allowed to ride all over the village on his bike. I'm the middle Austin and the ugly duckling. If I had more time to remember and think about it I'd be very sad. I'm skinny and as tall as the eight-year-olds and my legs are so long I keep falling. And I was awake early because this was a specially special December for me. I was to be the angel in the Pageant at church on Christmas Eve—the biggest and most wonderful thing that's ever happened to me. I was to wear a golden halo and a flowing white costume and wings, the loveliest wings anyone could imagine. Mother made them.

Suzy is four and she's the baby and all cuddly and beautiful and her hair is curly and the color of sunshine. She has great shining eyes that are the purple-blue of the sky just after sunset. She has a rosebud for a mouth, and she isn't skinny; she's just right.

We dressed quickly, because even if there wasn't any snow it was cold, and we ran downstairs just as John came in from delivering his papers, his cheeks shiny-red as apples from the cold. The dogs came running in after him, barking, Mr. Rochester, our big brindle Great Dane, and Colette, our little silver poodle. They're very good friends.

Our kitchen is a big wandery room that turns corners and has unexpected nooks and crannies. In the dining room section in the winter the fire crackles merrily, and this morning the smell of applewood mingled with the smell of pancakes and maple syrup and hot chocolate. One of the cats was sleeping, curled up on a cushion in front of the fire. Our father had already had his breakfast and gone out; he's a doctor and Mother said he'd gone out several hours ago to deliver a baby.

At that we looked at Mother, and the lovely bulge in her dress, and Mother smiled and said, "Daddy thinks the baby should come along sometime the first week of January."

"And then I won't be the baby any more!" Suzy said, "and I'll help you with the new baby."

Suzy's mind flits from thought to thought, just as she herself does, like a butterfly. Now she asked, "What's the surprise for the first day of December?"

It wasn't completely a surprise, because each year it's an Advent calendar, but it's partly a surprise, because it's always a new one. Advent means *coming*, and it's the four weeks that lead up to Christmas. Mother and Daddy read serious things in the evening, and talk about them, a book called *The Four Last Things*, for instance.

This year the calendar was a beautiful one, and had come all the way across the ocean, from Denmark. We take turns every day opening one of the windows to see what surprise picture is waiting behind. The twenty-fourth day when the windows open, they reveal the stable, and Mary and Joseph and the baby.

Today Suzy opened, because she's the youngest and goes first. Inside was a baby angel, who looked just like Suzy.

The next day, the second day of December, we all, even John, even Daddy when he got home from the office, made Christmas cookies. "We'd better make them early this year, just in case."

Just in case the baby comes early.

Mother added, "Babies have a way of keeping mothers too busy for Christmas cookies."

I was born at the end of November, so Mother didn't make any Christmas cookies that year. I always seem to spoil things. I looked out the long kitchen windows at the mountains, thinking: *Please, don't let me spoil anything this year. Don't let me spoil the Christmas Pageant. Help me to be a good angel. Please.*

On the third day of December after the school bus had let John and me off at the foot of the hill, and we'd trudged up the road to our house, Mother got wire and empty tin cans and a few Christmas tree balls. She took strong scissors and cut the tops and bottoms of the cans so that they made stars and curlicues. Then we took thread and hung the Christmas tree balls and the tin designs on the wire, and Mother and John balanced it, and we had made the most beautiful Christmas mobile you could possibly imagine. John got on the ladder and hung the mobile in the middle of the kitchen ceiling, and it turned and twirled and tinkled and twinkled.

The next day we looked for snow again, but the ground stayed brown, and the trees were dark against the sky. When we went out through the garage to walk down to the school bus, we looked at the big sled, at Daddy's snowshoes, at our ice skates hanging on the wall, at the skis. But though the wind was damp and we had on our warm Norwegian anoraks, we knew it wasn't cold enough for snow. The pond had a thin skin of ice, but not nearly enough for skating, and all that came down from the heavy grey skies was an occasional drizzle that John said might turn into sleet, but not snow.

And the days sped into December. On the fourth day Daddy put a big glimmering golden star over the mantelpiece in the living room. On the fifth day we taped a cardboard Santa Claus with his reindeer up the banisters of the front stairs; it came from England and is very bright and colorful. On the sixth day we strung the merry Norwegian elves across the whole length of the kitchen windows, and Mother said that our Christmas decorations were a real United Nations. On the seventh day we put a tall golden angel above the kitchen mantelpiece. Unlike the Advent calendar angel, this one was much too stately and dignified to look like Suzy, and I sighed because I knew that even with a costume and wings I could never hope to look as graceful and beautiful as the golden angel.

On the eighth day of December I was late getting home because the rehearsal of the pageant lasted much longer than usual. And it lasted longer because the director couldn't get me in a position that satisfied her. The most awful moment was when I heard her whisper to the assistant director, "I've never seen a seven-year-old be so awkward or ungraceful, but I suppose we really can't recast the angel now."

I clamped my teeth tight shut to try to keep from crying, and the director said, "Don't look so sullen, Vicky. An angel should be joyful, you know."

I nodded, but I didn't dare unclench my teeth. One tear slipped out and trickled down my cheek, but I didn't think anybody saw.

When the rehearsal was over, Mr. Quinn, the minister, drove me home. He hadn't seen the rehearsal and he kept talking about how the pageant was going to be the best ever, and that I was going to be a beautiful angel. If he'd been at the rehearsal he wouldn't have said that.

The Advent surprise for that day was to have the Christmas mugs at dinner, the mugs that look like Santa Claus. But I still felt like crying, and the cheerful Santa Claus face didn't cheer me up at all. After we had baths and were in our warm pajamas and ready for bed, we stood around the piano singing Advent carols, but I had such a big lump in my throat that I couldn't sing.

Daddy put his arm around me. "What's the matter with my girl?"

Two tears slipped out of my eyes, and I told him about the rehearsal and what the director had said. He told me that he and Mother would help me look and move more like an angel. "You can be a lovely angel, Vicky, but you'll have to work at it."

"I'll work. I promise."

On the ninth day of Advent we hung the Christmas bells from the beams in the living room, and then Mother worked with me on being an angel. She had me walk all over the house with a volume of the encyclopedia on my head. When I was finally able to walk all around without the encyclopedia falling, Mother showed me how to stand with my feet in ballet position, and how to hold my arms so they didn't look all elbows.

On the tenth day of December Mother got the cuddly Santa Claus doll out of the attic, and told Suzy and me we could take turns taking it to bed at night. I thought of the pageant, and said, "Suzy can have it. May I take the *Shu* to *Sub* volume of the encyclopedia to bed with me?"

Mother understood. "Yes. And now put it on your head and try walking up the front stairs and down the back stairs."

Each time I did it I managed more steps without having to catch the encyclopedia. Suzy went to bed with the cuddly Santa Claus doll. I put the *Shu* to *Sub* volume under my pillow.

On the eleventh day the director beamed at me and said, "That was *much* better, Vicky. I think you're going to be all right after all. Now let's try it again. *Good*, Vicky, GOOD."

I was happy when I got home and Mother gave me a hug, and John said, "I don't know why anybody ever thought you couldn't do it. I knew you could."

Suzy jumped up and down and said, "What're we going to do for Advent today?"

Mother suggested, "Let's make a Christmas chandelier." We took the wire mesh lettuce basket and filled it with the Christmas decorations which were just a tiny bit broken but not shattered. We hung one of the prettiest, shiniest decorations on the bottom of the lettuce basket, and then Mother and John fitted the basket over the front hall light so that it glittered and sparkled with the color of all the Christmas baubles.

And I walked up and down the front hall with the encyclopedia, *Shu* to *Sub*, balanced on my head; I tried to look at the Christmas chandelier out of the corner of my eye, but when I looked up the encyclopedia slipped and I caught it just before it landed on the floor.

On the twelfth day of December not only did it not snow, it did rain. Rain poured in great torrents from the sodden skies and the gutters spouted like fountains. After school Mother discovered that we'd eaten up all the first batch of Christmas cookies, so we made more.

On the thirteenth the skies were all washed clean and the sun was out and we had a pageant rehearsal. The director surprised me by saying, "Vicky, dear, you're doing so well that we've decided to give you some lines for the scene where you appear with the shepherds. Do you think you can memorize them?"

I nodded happily. It may be hard for me to walk without tripping up, and to stand still without being all sharp corners and angles, but memorizing things is easy for me.

The director explained, "These are the angel lines from an old play in the Chester Cycle. The Chester Cycle is a group of plays written in the Middle Ages in England, to be performed in the Cathedral in Chester, so we think it's very appropriate for the pageant. By the way, we miss your mother in the choir."

I explained, "It's because of the new baby, you know."

"Isn't that nice! I wonder if she'll be in the hospital for Christmas? Now here are your lines, dear. Read them slowly and clearly."

I read. Slowly and clearly. But I hardly heard myself. Mother in the hospital for Christmas? I knew Mother'd go to the hospital to have the baby, just as she did for John and me and Suzy. But not for Christmas Eve! Not for Christmas day!

"Good, dear," the director was saying, "Read it once more."

I read.

Shepherds, of this sight
Be not afright,
For this is God's night.
To Bethlehem now hie.
There shall ye see and sight

That Christ was born tonight
To save all mankind.

If Mother was in the hospital it wouldn't be Christmas. Christmas is the whole family hanging up stockings, and Daddy reading *The Night Before Christmas* and Saint Luke, and Mother singing everybody to sleep with her guitar and carols. What about the stocking presents Christmas morning in Mother's and Daddy's big bed? What about running downstairs all together to see the presents under the tree? What about—what about—everything?

Who would cook the Christmas dinner? Make the stuffing? Roast the turkey? Fix the cranberry sauce? What about putting out cocoa and cookies for Santa Claus the very last thing on Christmas Eve? What about—what about—everything?

"That's very good, dear," the director approved. "You speak beautifully. Now read it again, just a little bit more slowly this time. Do you think you can memorize it for tomorrow?"

I nodded numbly. Somehow or other I managed to do everything the director told me, but all I could think was—Mother *has* to be home for Christmas!

Daddy picked me up after rehearsal that afternoon. As soon as he had the car started, I asked, "Daddy, Mother isn't going to be in the hospital for Christmas is she?"

He answered quietly, "It's a distinct possibility."

I shouted, "But she can't be!"

Daddy said calmly, "According to our calculations, the baby's due about the first of January, but babies don't always arrive exactly on schedule. John, for instance, was three weeks late, and you were exactly on time. Suzy was a few days early."

"But—"

"Who knows, the baby may decide to come early enough so that Mother'll be home for Christmas. Or it mightn't be till the new year. But we have to accept the fact that there's a chance that Mother'll be in the hospital over Christmas."

"Let's not *have* the baby!" I cried. "If Mother has to be in the hospital on Christmas I don't want the baby! There are enough of us already." I choked over a sob. "Do we have to have the baby, Daddy?"

"Of course we do. We all want the baby. This isn't like you, Vicky Austin."

"What about Christmas dinner?" I wailed.

"At the last count," Daddy said, "we'd had seventeen invitations for dinner."

It kept getting worse and worse. "But we can't go out for Christmas dinner! I'd rather have cornflakes and have them at home!"

Daddy turned the car up the hill to the house. "I quite agree with you there, Vic. I've turned down all the invitations. If Mother's in the hospital I think you and John and Suzy and I can manage Christmas dinner, don't you? And I'll let you in on a secret: Mother already has a turkey stuffed and roasted and in the freezer. All we have to do is thaw it and heat it up in the oven."

I hiccuped tiredly. "Well. All right. But it won't be Christmas if Mother isn't with us."

Daddy changed the subject. He's very good about knowing when to do that. "I heard you saying your angel lines, Vicky. We're going to be very proud of you on Christmas Eve."

When we got home, Mother and John and Suzy were in the kitchen, stuffing dates. John shouted, "Vicky! There's snow forecast for tomorrow!"

On the fourteenth day of December three snowflakes fell. Exactly three. I counted them. They fell while we were out in the woods picking berries and ground pine for Christmas decorations.

On the fifteenth day of December Daddy and John got out the ladder, and Mother and Suzy and I untangled the long strings of outdoor lights and we trimmed the big Norway spruce.

"We're going to do quite a few things early this year," Daddy explained, "because of not knowing just when the baby is going to decide to be born." I didn't want to think about that.

At night the spruce shone so brightly that it could be seen all the way from the main road at the bottom of the hill.

And that afternoon Mother came to pick me up after rehearsal and the director said, just as though I couldn't hear, "I must admit to you, Mrs. Austin, that I was a little unsure of Vicky for the first few rehearsals. She's the youngest angel we've ever chosen and I had grave doubts as to whether or not she could do it. But now I think she's going to be the very best we've ever had, and she knows her lines perfectly."

One part of me blazed with happiness. Another part thought sadly—It won't be Christmas if Mother isn't home.

As we drove away from the church and turned down the main road, Mother pointed to the hilltop where our big white house perches, and I could see a little triangle of light that was the outdoor Christmas tree. And another awful thought struck me. "Mother! If you're in the hospital you won't be able to see me being the angel!"

"That's true."

"But I *want* you to see me!"

"I want to see you, too."

"In the olden days people didn't have to go to hospitals to have babies. They had them at home."

"So they did," Mother agreed. "But even if I had the baby at home, I couldn't come to see you being the angel."

"Why not?"

"Brand-new babies need a lot of attention," Mother said, "and they can't be taken out in the cold. I was pretty tied down at Christmas time the year you were born."

"But I was *born!*" I cried. "And you were home for Christmas. You didn't go off and leave John and Suzy alone. Oh, I forgot. Suzy wasn't born. Anyhow, Mother, please could you ask the baby to wait till after Christmas?"

"I can ask," Mother said, "but I wouldn't count on it. What shall we do today for our Special Thing?"

"Let's make the wreath for the front door."

"Good idea. We've got lots of ground pine and berries left over, and I saved all the pine cones we gilded and silvered last year. When we get home you can run up to the attic and get them."

On the sixteenth day of December John listened to the weather forecast before breakfast and snow was predicted again. The sky had the white look that means it is heavy with snow. John and I were so pleased we ran almost the whole of the mile down the hill to wait for the school bus. A cold raw wind was blowing and we huddled into our parkas.

After school I had a rehearsal. So did John, because he's singing in the choir, and this is the first time that the cast of the pageant and the choir have worked together.

I tried hard to walk the way I did with the *Shu* to *Sub* encyclopedia on my head, and to move my arms as though they were the graceful arms of a tree in December. I remembered all my lines in my heart as well as my mind, and Mother had worked with me to make each word ring out clear and pure as a bell. Everybody seemed pleased, and John pounded me on the back and told me I was a whiz. The choir director congratulated me, just as though I were a grownup, and told me that everybody was going to miss Mother in the choir, and I was forced once again to remember that Mother might not be home for Christmas. John asked the choir director if he thought it would snow, but he shook his head. "It's turned too cold for snow."

Mr. Irving, the choir director, drove us home and stopped in for a cup of tea. A big box of holly and mistletoe had arrived from our cousins on the West Coast, so John and Daddy hung the mistletoe on one of the beams in the living room.

After Mr. Irving had left, we opened the day's Christmas cards the way we always do, taking turns, so that each card can be looked at and admired and appreciated.

John remarked, "Some people just rip open their cards in the post office. I bet the kids never see them at all. I'm glad we don't do it that way."

"Everybody's different, John," Mother said. "That's what makes people interesting."

"Well, nobody else I know does something every day during Advent the way we do. What's our Special Thing for today?"

"Oh, I think the holly and the mistletoe's plenty. Start setting the table, Vic. It's nearly time to eat."

The days toward Christmas flew by, and still there was no snow. And no baby. And rehearsals went well and I was happy about the way being the angel was going, and so was the director.

On the seventeenth of December we hung our collection of doll angels all over the house, and on the eighteenth we put the Christmas candle in the big kitchen window. On the nineteenth we made Christmas cards, with colored paper and sparkle and cutouts from last year's Christmas cards.

On the twentieth we put up the crèche. This is one of the most special of all the special things that happen before Christmas. Over the kitchen counter is a cubby hole with two shelves. Usually mugs are kept in the bottom shelf, and the egg cups and the pitcher that is shaped like a cow on the top shelf. But for Christmas, Mother makes places for these in one of the kitchen cabinets. On the top shelf goes the wooden stable and the shepherds. Tiny wax angels fly over the stable. A dove sits on the roof. The ox and the ass and all the barnyard animals are put in, one by one, everybody taking turns. There is even a tiny pink pig with three little piglets, from a barnyard set John got one year for his birthday. There is a sheep dog and a setting hen and a grey elephant the size of the pig. Some people might think the elephant doesn't belong, but the year I was born Daddy gave him to John, and he's been part of the crèche ever since, along with two monkeys and a giraffe and a polar bear. Mary and Joseph will be put in on the morning of Christmas Eve, and then, when we get home from church on Christmas Eve night, Daddy puts in the baby Jesus, and reads the Nativity story from Saint Luke.

On the bottom shelf we put the wise men with their camels and their camel-keeper. We make a hill out of cotton, which is a little hard to balance the camels on, but when we're finished it really looks as though the train of camels was climbing up a long weary road towards the Christ child. On Twelfth Night they'll have finished their journey and join the shepherds and the animals in the stable.

Last of all Daddy put the star up above the stable and fixed the light behind it. On Christmas Eve we'll turn off all the other lights in the house, so all you can see is the lovely light from the star shining on the stable and the Holy Family and the angels and the animals.

On the twenty-first day of December we went with Daddy into the woods to get the Christmas tree. Mother stayed home, because she was feeling tired and heavy, but the rest of us tramped through the woods, including the dogs and cats. It was Suzy who found the perfect tree this time, just the right size and shape for the living room, with beautiful firm branches all around. Daddy and John took turns sawing, and we all help carry it home, because the tree was tall, and heavy.

Daddy said, "Tomorrow's Sunday, so we'll trim the tree a little ahead of time to get it ready for Santa Claus and to make sure Mother's here to help."

John asked, "You really don't think the baby's going to wait till after Christmas, Daddy?"

"I rather doubt it. Every indication is that this baby is going to be early. Now, kids, we'll put the tree carefully into the garage till tomorrow."

That night I woke up, very wide awake. I knew it wasn't anywhere near morning because the light was still on in Mother and Daddy's bedroom. After a few minutes I got up, softly, so as not to wake Suzy. I put on my bathrobe and slippers and tiptoed down to the kitchen. The dogs came pattering out to meet me, wagging their tails. One of the cats meowed at the head of the cellar stairs. I put my finger to my lips and said, "Shh! Everybody go back to sleep."

It wasn't quite dark in the kitchen because the embers in the fireplace were still glowing, and the night light was on. Mother and Daddy must have gone up to bed just a little while ago. I tiptoed over to the crèche, climbed on one of the kitchen stools, and turned on the light behind the star. The manger was empty, waiting for Mary and Joseph and the baby. They were still in their white cardboard box. I opened the lid and looked in, then closed the lid and put the box back.

Instead of feeling all full of anticipation the way I usually do, I felt heavy. I thought—I don't want Mother to be in the hospital for Christmas. I want her to be home. I'd give anything if she could be home. But I don't have anything to give. Anyhow. God doesn't expect us to give anything in order for him to love us. And least not a thing. Just ourselves.

I sighed again. And thought—Mother says we should never try to make bargains with God. That isn't the way God works. But I'd give up anything, even being the angel, if Mother could be home for Christmas.

I sat looking at the empty crib in the stable until I got sleepy.

On the twenty-second of December when we were all home from Sunday school and church, Mother made hamburgers and milk-shakes for lunch. Then Suzy and I helped with the dishes and Mother put on a carol record and we all sang "O Come, O Come Emmanuel." Daddy and John brought in the tree from the garage and set it firmly in a bucket of wet sand. The big boxes of Christmas decorations were brought down from the attic. First of all, Daddy got on the ladder and he and John put on the lights, and the angel at the top of the tree. The angel is wearing white, with feathery sparkly wings; it's the angel mother used to copy my costume. It was almost as though Daddy was putting a tiny *me* up on top of the tree.

I thought of the night before, and how I'd thought I'd be willing to give up being the angel if only Mother could be home for Christmas, but I couldn't give up being the angel without upsetting the whole Christmas pageant, and anyhow, that kind of thing isn't an offering to God. As our grandfather once told us, you can't offer anything less than yourself to God; anything less is a bribe, and bribing God is foolish, to say the least. I didn't really understand all of this. Grandfather's a theologian, though, and I was sure he was right.

Mother looked at me and said, "What's the matter, Vicky?"

"Nothing. May I put on some of the breakables this year?"

Suzy was given a box of unbreakable ornaments to go on the lowest branches of the tree. Mother smiled and handed me a beautiful little glass horn that really makes a musical sound. I blew it, and then I let Suzy blow it, too. We all worked together until the tree was shimmering with beauty.

I took a gold glass bell with a gentle tinkle and hung it on the highest branch I could reach. When the last decoration was hung from the tree and we'd all exclaimed (as usual) that it was the most beautiful tree ever, John ran around and turned out all the other lights so that the Christmas tree shone alone in the darkness. We all stood around it, very still, admiring it, and I was peaceful and happy. For a moment I forgot about being the angel. I even forgot about the baby.

On the twenty-third day of December when I went to the church for dress rehearsal, it finally began to snow. Everybody began to clap and shout with glee, and we kept running to the doors to look at the great feather flakes fluttering from a soft, fluffy sky. Finally the director got cross at us and ordered everyone inside, and Mr. Irving made a big discord on the organ.

In the Sunday school rooms several mothers helped us get into costume. I was dressed early, and Mrs. Irving, who dressed me, said, "Vicky dear, if you stand around here in this mob your wings are going to get crushed. Go sit quietly in the back of the church until we're ready to start the run-through."

I went, holding my wings carefully, through the big doors and half way down the nave. The church was transformed with pine boughs and candles. The candles wouldn't be lit until just before Christmas Eve service, but there was a spotlight shining on the manger. The girl who placed Mary came and stood beside me, a high school senior and very, very grown up. She wore a pale blue gown and a deep blue robe. She dropped one hand lightly on my shoulder.

"Some of us thought it was funny, such a little kid being chosen for the angel, and at first we thought you were going to be awful and ruin everything. But Mr. Quinn promised us you wouldn't, and now I think you're going to be the best thing in the pageant, I honestly do." Then she went and sat by the manger. She sat very still, her head bowed. She didn't seem like a high school senior any more. She seemed to belong in Bethlehem. Protecting my wings, I sat down in one of the pews. And for a while, I, too, seemed to be in Bethlehem.

Then the director called out time for the run-through to begin, and everything was hustle and bustle again. The choir in their red cassocks and white surplices lined up for the processional. I was shown into the corner behind the organ, from where I was to make my first entrance.

Everything went smoothly. I even managed to walk as though I had *Shu* to *Sub* on my head. My arms felt like curves instead of angles. My words were as bell-like as Mother'd been able to make them. At the final tableau I stood by the manger, and I felt shining with joy.

After the choir had recessed and the spotlight had faded on the Nativity scene, the director and Mr. Irving congratulated everybody. "It was beautiful, just beautiful!" The mothers who had helped with the costumes and had stayed to watch echoed, "Beautiful! Beautiful!" Except for the fathers, almost everybody who was going to be at church on Christmas Eve was already there.

The director gave me a big smile. "Vicky, you were just perfect.

Don't change one single thing. Tomorrow evening for the perform-ance do it just exactly the way you did today."

Daddy picked John and me up on his way home from the office. It was still snowing, great, heavy flakes. The ground was already white. Daddy said, "I'm glad I got those new snow tires after all."

John said, "You see, Daddy, we are going to have a white Christmas after all."

When we woke up on Christmas Eve morning, we ran to the win-dows. Not only was the ground white, but we couldn't even see the road. Mother said the snowplow went through at five o'clock so the farmers could get the milk out, and Daddy had followed the milk trucks, but the road had already filled in again.

We ate breakfast quickly, put on snowsuits, and ran out to play. The snow was soft and sticky, the very best kind for making snowmen and building forts. We spent the morning making a Christmas snow-man, and started a fort around him. John is good at cutting blocks out of snow like an Eskimo. We weren't nearly finished, though, when Mother called us in for lunch.

After lunch Suzy said, "I might as well go upstairs and have my nap and get it over with." We have to have naps on Christmas Eve if we want to stay after the pageant for the Christmas Eve service. Suzy is very businesslike about things like naps. Mother looked a little peculiar, but she didn't say anything, and Suzy went upstairs to bed, taking a book. She can't read, but she likes looking at pic-tures. Mother lit the kitchen fire and sat in front of it to read to John and me. We were just settled and comfortable when the phone rang. Mother answered it. We listened.

"Yes, I was afraid of that . . . Of course . . . They'll be disappointed, but they'll have to understand." She hung up and turned to John and me.

"What's the matter?" John asked.

Mother said, "The pageant's been called off because of the bliz-zard, and so has the Christmas Eve service."

"But *why?*" John demanded.

Mother looked out the windows. "How do you think anybody could travel in this weather, John? We're completely snowed in. The road men are concentrating on keeping the main roads open, but all the side roads are unusable. That means that about three quarters of the village is snowed in just like us. I'm sorry about the angel, Vicky. I know it's a big disappointment to you, but remember that lots of other children are disappointed, too."

I looked over at the crèche, with Mary and Joseph now in their places, and the manger still empty and waiting for the baby Jesus.

"Well, I guess lots worse things could happen." I thought—*If this means Mother will be home for Christmas . . .*

And then I thought—Blizzards can stop pageants, but they can't stop babies, and if the baby starts coming she'll have to go to the hospital anyhow . . .

"You're a good girl to be so philosophical," Mother said.

But I didn't really think I was being philosophical.

John said, "Anyhow, it looks as though the baby's going to wait till after Christmas."

Mother answered, "Let's hope so."

John pressed his nose against the window until the pane steamed up. "How's Daddy going to get home?"

It seemed to me that Mother looked anxious as she said, "I must admit I'm wondering about that myself."

"But it's Christmas Eve!" John said. "He has to get home!"

All Mother said was, "He'll do the best he can. At least I'm the only maternity case on his list right now."

In all my worrying about Mother not being home for Christmas, it had never occurred to me that Daddy mightn't be. Even when he's been called off on an emergency, he's always been around for most of the time. But if the blizzard was bad enough to call off church it was maybe bad enough so Daddy couldn't get up the long steep hill that led to the village.

When it began to get dark, Suzy woke up, all pink from sleep, and hurried downstairs. She was very cross when Mother told her that the pageant and the Christmas Eve service had been called off. "I needn't have slept so long after all! And I wanted to see Vicky be the angel!"

Mother answered, "We all did, Suzy."

Suzy stamped. "I'm mad at the old blizzard."

Mother laughed. "That's not going to stop the snow. And remember, you've been looking for snow every day. Now you've got it. With a vengeance. This is the worst blizzard I remember in years."

John lit the candle in the window and flicked the switch that turns on the outdoor Christmas tree and the light over the garage door. Then we all looked out the windows. The only way you could tell where the road used to be is by the five little pines at the edge of the lawn, and by the birches across the road. The outdoor Christmas tree was laden with snow, and the lights shone through and dropped small pools of color on the white ground. The great flakes of snow were still falling as heavily as ever, soft and starry against the darkness.

"I guess Daddy'll have to spend the night at the hospital," John said.

Mother came to the window and looked over our heads. "No car can possibly get up that road."

Suzy asked, "What're we going to have for dinner?"

Mother turned from the window. "I think I'll just take hamburger out of the freezer . . ." I thought she looked worried.

I stayed by the window.—*Please let Daddy get home. Please let Daddy get home.*

But I knew Mother was right, and a car couldn't possibly get up the road, even with new snow tires and chains.

—*Please, God, I'm not bargaining, I'm not bribing or anything, I'm just asking, Please let Daddy get home. If I knew how to offer my whole self I would, but I don't know how, so please let Daddy get home, please let . . .*

Then, just as the words began to jumble themselves up in my mind, I saw something in the wide expanse of snow, somewhere near where the curve of the road ought to be. A light. "Mother! John! Suzy!" They all came running to the window.

"It's a flashlight!" John said.

"Snowshoes!" Mother cried. "John, run to the garage and see if Daddy took his snowshoes!"

John hurried to the kitchen door and in a minute came back, grinning happily. "They're gone."

The light came closer and closer and soon we could see Daddy, his head and shoulders covered with snow. His snowshoes moved steadily and regularly over the white ground. We ran tumbling out to the garage and flung our arms around him, and the dogs jumped up on him and barked in greeting.

"Whoa!" he said. "Let me get my snowshoes off!" He handed the snowshoes to John, who hung them up. Then he stamped his feet and shook, and snow tumbled off him. The dogs dashed out into the snow, came whirling back into the garage, and shook off even more snow. "Come along," Daddy said. "Let's get in out of the cold."

When we got indoors Daddy kissed Mother. She leaned her head against his shoulder. "I was afraid you wouldn't be able to get home."

Daddy said, "You didn't think I'd leave you now, did you?"

And Mother said, "I've been having contractions off and on all day. Oh, I am so glad you're home!"

Daddy put another log on the fire. Outdoors the snow was still falling. Indoors it was warm and cozy. The star lit up the little stable, and Daddy went to the white cardboard box and took out the tiny wax figure of the baby. "I think we can put him the manger, now."

Mother said, "We might as well have the reading, now, too, because this is all the Christmas Eve service we're going to get."

John went into the living room and turned on the Christmas tree lights so that there was the beauty of the Christmas tree indoors and the Christmas tree outdoors, and Daddy sat by the fire and read us the Christmas story. I looked at the angel on top of the indoor Christmas tree and I felt peaceful and happy.

When we'd finished dinner and were nearly through with the dishes, Mother gave a funny little gasp and said to Daddy, "How are you going to get me to the hospital?"

Daddy laughed. "Upstairs is as far as I'm going to get you tonight." He looked at us. "Children, I'm going to ask you to finish the dishes and clean up the kitchen." Suddenly he sounded like a doctor, not just Daddy. "John, put on a full kettle to boil. Blizzards don't ask anybody when they should come, and neither do babies."

He put his arm about Mother and they went upstairs.

"What about dessert?" Suzy asked. "We were going to have dessert after we'd done the dishes."

"If you're really interested in dessert, I'll get you some ice cream out of the freezer," John said.

After all, Suzy is a very little girl. She ate a large bowl of ice cream.

When the kitchen was all cleaned up, Daddy came downstairs. He carried the Christmas stockings and he told us to hang them carefully at the living room fireplace. "You'd be staying up late tonight anyhow, so please just be good. Vicky, keep that kettle hot for me, and feed the cats and put them down in the cellar for the night."

The snow beat against the windows. The wind rattled the shutters. In spite of her nap Suzy got sleepy and curled up on the living room sofa. I went to the stove. "I'd better make the cocoa to put on the mantelpiece with the cookies for Santa Claus."

"Make enough for us while you're at it," John said.

We drank two, then three cups of cocoa. We tiptoed out to the storeroom where we'd hidden our presents for Mother and Daddy and put them under the tree. Time seemed to stretch out and out and Daddy didn't come back downstairs. The dogs lay in front of the fire and snored. Suddenly Mr. Rochester, the Great Dane, pricked up his ears. John and I listened, but we didn't hear anything. At the top of the cellar stairs a cat meowed. Mr. Rochester sat up and raised his head; his tail thumped against the floor.

Then we did hear something, something unmistakable, loud and clear. A cry. A baby's cry.

I started to get up, but John said, "Wait."

In a little while Daddy came bounding down the stairs. He was beaming. "You have a little brother, children!" He took the kettle and hurried back up the stairs, calling, "You can come up in a few minutes. Wait."

The baby cried again, a lusty yell.

I went to the crêche. The light from the star shone down on the stable. The elephant and the pig and her piglets seemed to have moved in closer. The baby lay on his bed of straw.

"Listen." John held up his hand. Across the fields came the sound of the clock in the church steeple striking midnight. "Let's wake Suzy up, and tell her."

Suzy sleeps soundly and it took us a long time to wake her properly. By the time she realized what had happened, Daddy came back downstairs.

"You can come up now, for just a minute, children. But Mother's tired, and the baby's asleep, so be very quiet."

We tiptoed up the stairs and into the big bedroom. Mother was lying in the big bed and smiling. In the crook of her arm was little bundle. We tiptoed closer. The bundle was our baby brother. His face was all puckered and rosy. His eyes were closed tight. He had a wisp of dampish hair. He had a tiny bud of a mouth. One little fist was close to his cheek. We stood and stared at him. We were too excited and awed to speak.

Mother asked, "Isn't he beautiful?" and we all nodded.

Then Daddy shooed us out. "All right. Time for bed, everybody."

John went off to his room, and Suzy and I to ours. When we had undressed and brushed our teeth and Suzy was in bed, I stood at the window. The snow had stopped. The ground was a great soft blanket of white, broken by the dark lines of trees and the gay colors of the outdoor tree. The sky was dark and clear and crusted with stars. I watched and watched and there was one star that was brighter and more sparkling than any of the others.

The Christmas star.

Mother was home. Daddy was home. Our baby brother was home. We were all together.

I whispered, "Thank you."

And the light shone right into my heart.

Acknowledgments

Some of the pieces in this book are previously unpublished and are used by kind permission of Madeleine L'Engle.

Grateful acknowledgment is made to the following publishers for permission to use these works:

"Joyful in the newness of the heart" from *The Anglican Digest* (Pentecost, 1983). Reprinted by permission.

"Redeeming All Brokenness" and "Revealing Structure," from Madeleine L'Engle's introduction to *Awaiting the Child: An Advent Journal* by Isabel Anders. Copyright © 1987 by Isabel Anders Throop. Reprinted by permission of Isabel Anders.

"'Anesthetics,'" from A CIRCLE OF QUIET. Copyright © 1972 by Crosswicks, Ltd. Reprinted by permission of Farrar, Straus & Giroux, Inc.

"This Extraordinary Birth," "Forever's start," "After annunciation," "A Galaxy, a Baby," "That Newness," "The promise of his birth," "In Human Flesh," "The birth of wonder," "A Time of Hope," "The Eve of Epiphany," "The Light of the Stars," "Atomic Furnaces," "Soaring," from THE IRRATIONAL SEASON. Copyright © 1977 by Crosswicks, Ltd. Reprinted by permission of HarperCollins Publishers, Inc.

"Miracle on 10th Street," from *Life* (December 1991). Reprinted by permission of the author.

"This tiny baby" (from "The Baby in the Bath"), "Tree at Christmas," "For Dana" (originally titled "For Dana: 4th November"), from LINES SCRIBBLED ON AN ENVELOPE. Copyright © 1969 by Crosswicks, Ltd. Used by permission of Farrar, Straus & Giroux, Inc.

"A Full House: An Austin Family Story" (originally titled "A Full House"), from *McCall's* (December 1980). Reprinted by permission of the author.

The poem contained in "The Glorious Mystery" beginning, "This is no time for a child to be born" was previously published as "The Risk of Birth" in *The Risk of Birth*, copyright © 1974 by Harold Shaw Publishers. Used by permission.

"Transfiguration" from *Stories for the Christian Year*. Copyright © 1992 by The Chrysostom Society. Used by permission of Macmillan Publishing Company.

"Eighty-second Street," "Chamonix," "Saying Yes," "A Deepening Vision," from THE SUMMER OF THE GREAT-GRANDMOTHER. Copyright © 1974 by Crosswicks, Ltd. Used by permission of Farrar, Straus & Giroux, Inc.

"The Twenty-Four Days Before Christmas: An Austin Family Story" is a reprint of the book by the same title, copyright © 1984 by Crosswicks, Ltd. Used by permission of Harold Shaw Publishers.

Selections from the following books by Madeleine L'Engle used by permission of Harold Shaw Publishers: *Anytime Prayers, A Cry like a Bell, Penguins and Golden Calves, The Rock That Is Higher, Sold into Egypt, A Stone for a Pillow, Walking on Water,* and *The Weather of the Heart.*

Thanks also to the Wheaton College Special Collections for providing many of the materials used in this book.

We have sought to secure permissions for all copyrighted material in this book. Where acknowledgment was inadvertently omitted, the publisher expresses regret.